ALEKS KROTOSKI

UNTANGLING THE WEB

WHAT THE INTERNET IS DOING TO YOU

First published in 2013
by Faber and Faber Limited
Bloomsbury House
74–77 Great Russell Street
London WC1B 3DA

Published with Guardian Books
Guardian Books is an imprint of Guardian Newspapers Ltd
www.guardianbooks.co.uk

Typeset by seagulls.net
Printed in England by CPI Group (UK) Ltd, Croydon, CR0 4YY

A CIP record for this book is available from the British Library

ISBN 978-0-571-30366-3

FSC
www.fsc.org
MIX
Paper from
responsible sources
FSC® C008047

10 9 8 7 6 5 4 3 2 1

UNTANGLING THE WEB

This book is to be returned on or before
the last date stamped below.

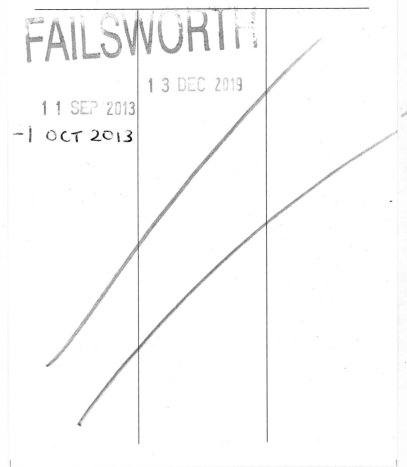

FAILSWORTH

1 3 DEC 2019

1 1 SEP 2013

-1 OCT 2013

CONTENTS

ACKNOWLEDGEMENTS

This book is the product of thirteen years of research, as a journalist and as an academic. The chapters have appeared, some in more similar guises than others, in the *Observer* and the *Guardian*, on the BBC website, on BBC Two's *The Virtual Revolution*, on Radio 4's *Digital Human*, on the Digital Media and Learning blog and in *The Political Quarterly*. Some had their first iterations as lectures at the University of Oxford, the University of Cambridge, the London School of Economics, the University of Glasgow, the University of Nottingham, *The Economist*, Google, the Royal Institution and the Internet Advertising Bureau. They've been presented to audiences from the UK, the US, Singapore, Taiwan, the Netherlands, Australia, Greece, Denmark, Belgium and France. Most importantly to my personal sense of completion, several chapters have been adapted from my PhD.

It is, therefore, unsurprising that there are many people who contributed to these pages. I'd like to thank my editors Katie Roden, Charles Arthur, Caspar Llewellyn-Smith, Killian Fox, Ian Tucker and Phil Daoust for harnessing my verbosity; my research supervisors Julie Barnett and Evanthia Lyons for keeping me on target; my parents Danuta and Wojciech for their continuing and enduring support; my friends Amber Templemore-Finlayson, Devina Sivagurunathan, Marie Campbell, Kate Bevan, Sam Pinney, Denise Hanrahan, Roslyn Smith and Kaitlin Thaney for reading early versions of these chapters; Gregor and Ally McMurtrie for the loan of their home in idyllic Findochty, Scotland to hammer out draft two; and Ben Hammersley for helping me cross the finish line.

INTRODUCTION

More than two billion people, from Peterborough to Pretoria, from Toronto to Timbuktu, from Amsterdam to Abu Dhabi, use the world wide web. There are over 2.5 billion searches for information and insight on Google every day. Nine hundred million of us connect and share on the world's largest social network, Facebook. More than 500 million of us tell friends, lovers, strangers and stalkers what we had for breakfast on Twitter. And when we want to shop for books or balalaikas, hundreds of millions more point our browsers at Amazon and eBay. In just two decades the web has become inextricably tangled into the fabric of our lives.

In the UK, the government has poured billions of pounds into getting people connected. Already, 82.9% of the adult population has used the internet at least once. All our essential services – from ordering library books to getting a driver's licence to voting for our local councillors – are being moved into virtuality. Like it or not, soon everyone will have to be online.

Many of us don't like this, however. We fear it. We don't understand it. We think the technology is replacing us at work, diluting our communities, stealing away our children, upending morality, taking control of our lives. We read about online cults and internet extremism, about cyber-infidelity and computer addiction, about fraud, identity theft and antisocial behaviour. We are afraid this new worldwide order is taking something essentially human away from us.

At the same time, we are bombarded with headlines that claim this communication technology is a panacea. We see stories of how the web has been harnessed to topple corrupt governments, to transform media empires, to empower people just like us to do exceptional things.

With so much information coming from so many sides at such a pace, it's no wonder we're confused. No wonder that, in taxis, on trains, in pubs, over dinner, in companies and in government offices, you'll hear people asking: what is the web doing to us, to our kids, to society? What can we do to harness it? Should it be stopped? Can it be?

The web is under furious scrutiny from scientists and academics too. At Tel Aviv University, for instance, Dr Katelyn McKenna has spent most of her career investigating claims that the web is making us antisocial. At MIT and the University of Amsterdam, Professor Sherry Turkle and Dr Tom Postmes have spent 20 years looking at the effects of online anonymity. And at Sheffield Hallam University, Dr Feona Attwood has analysed how the web has affected our attitudes to sex, and how different our bedroom behaviours are since the advent of networked technologies like "teledildonics" and easy access to pornography. Much of this valuable research is hidden behind the walls of the ivory tower, however. All too often, public debate is fuelled by nothing but half-truths and misunderstandings. As a result, our access to the web is threatened by groups that want to regulate it and shut it down, and they are winning hearts and minds with misinformation.

What's lacking in this battle is evidence, and that's where this book comes in. I have done time inside the ivory tower. I am part of the internet research community and have been for over a decade; my PhD looked at the psychology of online communities, and my current focus is on what it means to put our faith in the machine. I've also spent the last 15 years as a technology journalist for the BBC and the Guardian, translating web science into a language that can be understood outside academia. As well as the scientists mentioned above, I have interviewed everyone from Sir Tim Berners-Lee, founder of the world wide web, to Mark Zuckerberg, founder of Facebook. I've spoken with developers who want to solve world hunger, inequality and death, and with bloggers who simply want to make people laugh.

In the pages that follow, I'll attempt to untangle the unfounded claims, the rumours and the scaremongering about the web from the reality. In the first section, "Untangling me", I'll talk about how this new technology affects our minds and our bodies – from sickness and health to sex and death. As we lean on it for information about ourselves, we also upload valuable information that will be useful after we die. Can we live forever? Should we want to? And what does the way we use the web say about what we value about us and each other? In the second section, "Untangling us", I'll unpick the modern meaning of family, home and the neighbourhood. Do we love and hate in the same way that we always have done, or is something new going on? I'll also take a look at what the web is doing to our kids. Finally, in the third section, "Untangling society", you'll get the lowdown on the biggest questions of all. How is the web upending modern society? Will it lead to a global social revolution, or is the government already using it to control us? Are we losing our national identities and culture, and what has changed about what we believe in?

The book ends with a look at an issue that's beginning to make its way into conversations: who is *designing* the web? How are these men and women in technology hubs from Silicon Valley in San Francisco to Silicon Roundabout in London creating a clever and thoughtful computerised service that address our needs, when all they have to play with is binary computer code? What do the motivations of the

21st-century human being look like? And what would a human being created by the web want and need?

Everyone is now familiar enough with the web to have an opinion about it, but no one really knows whether they're right or wrong. What is the new information revolution really doing to us? In this book, you'll find out.

UNTANGLING ME

In the spring of 1996, an enterprising American college student named Jennifer Ringley connected a webcam to her computer and began seven years of uninterrupted self-exposure. JenniCAM, as she eventually named it, was the first no-holds-barred lifelogging experiment on the world wide web. Every 15 seconds, the webcam uploaded another still image – from the mundane to the erotic – exposing the uncensored life of a young woman coming of age.

The web at the time of JenniCAM was still in its infancy: this was before Google made it navigable, before the dotcom bubble began to inflate, and before Facebook CEO Mark Zuckerberg was out of short trousers. Compared with the modern world of universal broadband access, instant feedback and streaming video, it was achingly slow: websites with pictures took entire minutes to download, and publishing anything required expert knowledge in at least one computer language.

JenniCAM represented our self-aware future, the place we inhabit in the second decade of the 21st century, now that 82% of American adults use the web, and the average amount of time we spend online doubles every five years. We are in an era when 800 million people from around the world peek into real lives via YouTube every month to watch the more than 72 hours of video we upload every second. We have evolved into the people that JenniCAM represented: both the voyeur and the viewed, playing with what we perceive to be our audience's notions of who we are. The controversy over Ringley's brash experiment is mirrored by the headlines we read almost two decades later about the effects of online life. Then, the Wall Street Journal described Ringley as a narcissist fantasist, while the LA Times called JenniCAM "so straightforward it's warped, so simple it's complex, so humbling it's audacious, so plain it's creative, so worldly it's innocent". Now, we have stories headed "Facebook's 'dark side': study finds link to socially aggressive narcissism".

Public displays of the self haven't disappeared into the history of the network as embarrassing experiments in self-promotion – our mass migration online has only encouraged them. We flood the web with personal information: status updates, personal opinions, intentions, pictures and videos. Sixteen years after Ringley turned her camera on, we now tell our Facebook friends when we're single or engaged or hungover and hate our jobs at a rate of 30 billion updates a month. We tell people when we're out of the house and what we've bought, practically begging people to steal our stuff. We post private phone numbers in public places, tell anyone what we had for breakfast and share secrets about our friends with the rest of the world. Is the online population stuck in an infantile culture of attention seeking? Does the web give us an entirely new opportunity to steal, stalk and seduce, as we lay bare our whereabouts, feelings and interests for public consumption? Or are we now in the ultimate identity laboratory: a place where we can redefine who we are, who we were, and who we might become?

A NATION OF NARCISSISTS

If you stick my name – or, indeed, any similar collection of As, Ks, Ss and Ts – into Google you'll discover a hefty archive of digital stuff about "Aleks Krotoski" from around 1999. That was the year I began presenting a television programme about computer games. Perhaps because this was a subject that appealed to a technologically proficient demographic, the day after the show first broadcast on Channel 4, I woke up to discover photos, videos and sites about myself and my two co-presenters plastered all over the web. Pieces of my past and present were suddenly out there. I was documented and published, and I had no say at all in how I was being presented. I felt winded, vulnerable. Overnight, I'd lost my grip on who I thought I was. I was no longer in charge. I could be taken out of context by anyone with an internet connection, and I could do nothing about it.

Or could I? The online Aleks Krotoski was actually only a part of my identity, and one that was shaped by people who had the skills to put stuff up there. I figured I could still have control over "me", by playing them at their own game. And so, since that time, I've used an offensive strategy that involves flooding the web with information about myself, from my point of view.

It's my way of re-establishing control over Aleks Krotoski, the online identity. Most of what I put out there is a carefully curated selection of professional and personal information that generally shows me in a good light. Even the terrible photos I took of myself and published on Flickr when I was in the desperate final throes of writing my PhD (and those I'm currently taking while writing this book) demonstrate a positive side of my identity: they lead, ultimately, to a conclusion in which I progress, and progress well. In other words, they document the process, warts and all, of a Super Me. And my hope is that the warts that I leave behind – or that others put online about me – will be placed in context. Or forgotten.

What I'm doing isn't particularly narcissistic or unusual: there are more than 140 million updates added each day to microblogging service Twitter – which has archived more than 30 billion tweets in the US Library of Congress – and more than one billion people publish photos on Facebook for their friends and family to see. Our motivations for doing this are to document and archive, to preserve and promote identity. To perform the part of "me" in the theatre of life for an audience of friends, family, lovers and strangers, and express who we are.

But is my collection of status updates, photos, videos, blogposts and podcasts really me? It's one expression of self, for sure. It's also one that I manipulate. When my Twitter feed was described by a British national newspaper as "disjointed, yet fascinating", I took this to mean that they thought I was having a breakdown, and so I upped the disjointedness for laughs. The response from both friends and strangers was remarkable: I had to assure them I was OK, and that I was playing – as I only could online – with my identity. Many were angry that I was messing with their perceptions of who I was by manipulating who I professed to be.

More interesting are the accounts I have on other networks that are totally unrelated to my "Aleks Krotoski" identity. They're not anonymous to the people in those communities: I've been an active member posting under the same pseudonym for over a decade, and the people there know me under that identity. That's a different expression of self, one

that psychologists and web theorists believe is incredibly valuable to
our personal development, but one that is increasingly under threat.

There are many theories about how we develop our identities, both
in childhood and as adults. Underpinning them all is the idea that
we decide if something is or isn't "us", depending on whether or not
it makes us feel good about ourselves. We're driven by positive self-
esteem: if we're comfortable in our own skins, we can stride forth in
our everyday lives with the confidence that we will be true to ourselves
even when battered by the little and large things that life throws at us.
But as anyone who's gone through the teenage years can attest, getting
to that level of self-confidence can be awfully painful. Settling into an
accurate definition of the self requires trying on a lot of inappropriate
identities and making a lot of mistakes. Again and again, by stumbling
and falling and getting up again, we redefine ourselves into something
that we eventually become content with. For this, though, we need to be
aware of all the possibilities so we can try them on to see if they fit, and
we need to have the freedom to fail without devastating personal and
social consequences. And this is where the web comes in.

MIT professor Sherry Turkle is a whirlwind of a woman. Pint-sized,
fiercely ambitious and bursting with energy, she has been a practising
psychoanalyst and internet identity researcher for over two decades.
More than anyone else in my career, it is Turkle who has caused me
to quake in my boots every time we've met. "The imperative to self-
knowledge has always been at the heart of philosophical inquiry," she
wrote in the seminal book about the web and the self, *Life on the Screen:
Identity in the Age of the Internet*. Published in 1995 as the second part
of a trilogy that looked at our relationships with technology, it was the
go-to guide for many researchers for more than a decade, describing

how we think about who we are in online spaces, and what that means for us offline. At the time that *Life on the Screen* came out, the freaks and geeks populating the internet's tubes were a specialised bunch; most were college students and their professors, hailing from a remarkably small talent pool and geographical area. Tech-savvy and generally open-minded, they were more than willing to embrace the unprecedented fluidity of self-expression that this new technology afforded.

Turkle argued that two things about the web had an important impact on our sense of identity: its default anonymity, which allowed its digital residents to try on new skins, and the ability to compartmentalise these in different, unrelated virtual communities. "Play has always been an important aspect of our individual efforts to build identity," she said, referencing developmental psychologist Erik Erikson, and nodding to the theories of psychoanalysts Sigmund Freud, Jacques Lacan and Carl Jung. "In terms of our views of the self, new images of multiplicity, heterogeneity, flexibility and fragmentation dominate the current thinking about human identity."

Contrary to its Latin root, identity need not mean "the same", she argued. "No one aspect can be claimed as the absolute 'true self'," she wrote, since the web gives us the opportunity to get to know our "inner diversity". In the great psychoanalytic tradition, she said that in order to achieve self-actualisation – in other words, to "be all you truly feel you can be" – we must come to terms with who we are, and integrate each aspect of it into a coherent whole.

The web fits this postmodern concept of the self perfectly. Identity is prismatic and multiplicitous, context-dependent and subjective. It allows us to be inventive and creative in how we express who we are and who we want to be. I can be "@aleksk", playing up the "disjointed, yet fascinating" personality on Twitter, "Aleks Krotoski", the researcher who writes about social psychology and the web, and "toastwife" on Flickr, where I share George Orwell-themed photographs. As a psychoanalyst and web user herself, Turkle spent much of the book explaining why the articulation of multiple "personalities" wasn't unhealthy, despite a growing concern among the popular press that somehow we were becoming fragmented by using the web, and losing our grip on reality.

In fact, as a group of researchers at New York University were discovering around the same time Turkle published *Life on the Screen*, the web was helping people to self-actualise. As more and more people were going online, researchers John Bargh and Katelyn McKenna were interviewing people who tried on virtual identities that they felt they couldn't share with offline friends and family. In one study, just as the tech bubble was beginning to inflate in 1998, they spoke with gay men who were still in the closet offline, but who were exploring their gay identities by talking through their feelings and experiences in an online forum. Over time, and through the support of fellow community members, many felt comfortable enough to integrate this new, challenging identity into their sense of self, and to eventually bring it offline. Because they had practised virtually, they were able to deal with the consequences of an identity shift in their original social worlds.

There are many other similar stories. I've interviewed people who have developed confidence in their offline abilities to organise and hold a crowd because they've led groups in online games. I've spoken with gamers with severe physical disabilities who adopt very physical personas online, and they have told me how their digital roles made them feel more confident in their own abilities, and what they thought they were capable of in their offline worlds. What the web does so well is give a person the opportunity to separate the social categories we belong to, like being female, a mother, a volleyball player, Norwegian, liberal or

Catholic, from the personal categories we feel, like our subjective sense of who we feel we are. Contrary to Turkle's problem with the single "true" self, McKenna and Bargh and their colleagues were finding that, online, people said they were able to express a "true" self: a little piece of who they really were. They were able to say things they felt unable to say in their usual circles, just as they might do with a stranger they met on a train. They might be able to express themselves in a way that felt closer to who they felt they were. This is something we all do when we go online. Even if you've never ventured into an online game or been a signed-up member of a web community, you've probably developed a profile for a social network, written a blog, commented on an article or contributed to the ongoing flood of updates on Twitter. You may have done more than one of these. Congratulations: you have created a virtual "you".

What makes the web so exciting is the potential to make that "you" different from who you are offline. So what if you, as a man, decide to explore your feminine side by choosing a female avatar in an online game? Or if you, as a disabled person, want to find out what it's like to be in a community when no one knows you use a wheelchair? Are you deceiving them? Are you being untruthful? Or are you simply putting yourself in another person's shoes to the best of your ability? And what if you just want to start from scratch, to reinvent a part of yourself in a different context, where no one will make assumptions about who you are based on or who you've been?

I used to be able to completely reinvent myself once every five years. That's on average how often I've moved cities. I started life on the road a week after I was born on a round-the-world trip that was part of my father's work, and I've not been able to settle down since.

This gave me a powerful sense of control over how others perceive me. I was able to explore something new about myself in every new place, and leave behind the history that I chose not to share with my new friends. I wasn't escaping anything by not sharing, nor was I deceiving anyone; some things never come up. The Aleks I was in Louisiana was different from the Aleks I was in Washington DC, who was different from the Aleks I was in Glasgow, who was different from the Aleks I was in Brighton. And these were different from the Aleks I was when I was on holiday in Spain last year. But the web has eroded all of that. My online identity is a consistent, never-relenting backlog of "stuff" that I cannot get rid of, that – crucially – other people can see and that therefore I am accountable for even if I move to another city, country or planet. Because of my persistent online self, I, Aleks Krotoski, can no longer start over. This is a weird vulnerability that I'm not used to: when I'm looking for a job, an apartment to rent or a date, a quick Google search will uncover a trail of information about me and my past that I've put up and others have put up about me. It's as if all my frequent flier miles have disappeared and I can never be anonymous or faceless again.

Of course, not everyone has been as mobile as I have. Most people stay in one place and experience the longevity of identity, then struggle to reinvent themselves within their intimate circles. But now the web has become my too-close community, my personal small town.

And the reason? Unlike the web Sherry Turkle, Katelyn McKenna and John Bargh wrote about in the 1990s, there's a new trend in web identity: we're losing the ability to be anyone online.

A friend of mine has had the same online name since 1994. It is her consistent, persistent online handle, and she is known by it in communities who have no idea who she is offline. She chose the pseudonym when she was starting her PhD research into online communities, and over time she became well known within her circle of virtual friends. Her online name became a kind of public persona. Until recently, she managed to keep it so separate from her offline self that if you typed her real name into Google, her pseudonymous blog, Flickr account and other online activity were nowhere to be seen. She never made a choice to be anonymous; the self she expressed when using that online handle was who she was in that context. It happened to be different from her work self, or the self she showed to her family. We all do it offline, it's just that now we do it in public and it's saved in perpetuity, online.

This friend set up a Facebook account in 2005 under her pseudonym and used it intensely for two years. Then one day her profile page broke, so she contacted customer services. Without warning, they deleted her account for breaching the terms of service: she had created a Facebook profile that didn't appear to be under her real name. "How dare you make the decision that's not my real name?" she emailed them. They were immovable. Her online self was not real, they said, despite its decade and a half of history. It's as if an entire chapter of her life had been erased. "I really resented that assumption," she told me later. "My identity is not a nickname or an impostor: at that time, I had used that pseudonym for over ten years. It's a right to have a different online identity." She has since also been ejected from Google's social network, Google+, for using the same online handle. "I think it's fundamentally wrong," she says. "I refuse to re-establish two decades of who I am because they have an idea about what a name looks like."

This is not an isolated case. The old web, a place where identity could remain separate from real life, is rapidly disappearing. According to Sheryl Sandberg, Facebook's chief operating officer, and Richard Allan, its director of policy in Europe, people who have arrived on the web since 2003 only want online interactions supported by "authentic" identity. And this "authentic" identity is incompatible with pseudonyms, however well established. Facebook profiles and Google IDs are automatically tied into a person's real name and real connections, and to all activities across cyberspace. You log into other services using Facebook or Google IDs, and this forces a single public identity that's an aggregated version of your offline past and online present.

"I would not call what you have on Facebook 'authentic' identity," says Christopher Poole, the 24-year-old creator of 4Chan, a 20-million strong community founded in 2004. 4Chan boasts two design features antithetical to Facebook and other single-identity online services: first, its users don't register an account to participate and are therefore anonymous to one another; second, there's no archive. Nothing is retained. Ever. Poole, who was voted *Time*'s most influential person of 2008, thinks Facebook's approach ignores the diversity of human experience and shuts down the online experience. "Mark [Zuckerberg] and Sheryl [Sandberg] have gone out and said that identity is authenticity, that you are online who you are offline, and to have multiple identities is lacking in integrity. I think that's nuts," he says. "Individuals are multifaceted. Identity is prismatic."

According to Richard Allan, however, what the millions who have come online over the last decade actually want is a safe place where they won't experience bad behaviour, have their identities stolen or be duped by impostors. Although the first decade of the web was indeed characterised by pseudonyms developed over time in intimate environments, Allan believes that "pretend identities don't work very well now that the web has moved from a minority sport for geeks to a mainstream occupation."

Yet a modern social network's success doesn't need to rely on a direct link between online and offline identity. In Japan, the three most popular social networks ask users to create pseudonyms, as do the two most popular mobile social networks in India. In both cases, these systems work because of offline social restrictions. "Because the relationships between superiors and inferiors are very strict in Japan and people fear social isolation, Japanese people don't assert their opinions clearly offline," says Yasutaka Yuno, editor-in-chief of one of Japan's most popular tech magazines, *K-tai Watch*. "Of course, people have their own opinions, and anonymous social network services allow them to say them." In India, meanwhile, the pseudonyms people use on social networks like Mig33 and RocketTalk let them connect across the caste system on the basis of interest rather than birthright. Even in countries where social network account holders are required to register for services using a national ID, such as South Korea and China, people can still use pseudonyms or lie about their personal demographic features like age, sex or location. Users continue to play with identity, despite knowing their activities are traceable.

The most important feature of anonymity for identity, according to Andrew Lewman, executive director of the Tor Project, is "the ability to forget, to start over". Tor software makes users' locations and online activities untraceable, which means you have no persistent, centralised identity that a commercial service can use to identify you. "Maybe you just got divorced, maybe you just came out of rehab and you want to start over. As soon as you log into a Gmail account, you start getting ads for the drug rehab you want to forget. If you're in a real-name environment, such as Facebook, unless you actually physically change your name and your friends, you're thrown right back into your old life." Although Facebook does allow users to curate what's public and private – "recasting your public persona by selecting from the data you've put onto the service", as Allan puts it – Lewman believes the automated systems make a total social reinvention difficult to pull off.

Now that there are so many ways to publish and share pictures, videos and text with friends, family, workmates, classmates and strangers, we all have a platform to express ourselves. Today's web is splattered with information about who we are, but this comes at a price. While the old web let us play with our identities, this kind of activity is increasingly under threat, and the prognosis is that this isn't going to go away. In fact, quite the reverse. The hold-outs of anonymity online are fewer and further between, making us more accountable across space and time for the decisions we make now for who we will be later on.

There are very few things that are different now from before we went online, but identity is one that's become entangled by our online lives. We can now express ourselves more fully than ever before, but the price we pay is that we can now no longer disappear.

LIFE AFTER DEATH

Towards the end of my psychology degree in the States, I enrolled in "Death Studies", a summer course about the psychological, social and medical issues that surround the end of life. The first thing drummed into the students by the professor, the now deceased Dan Leviton, was a philosophical tenet: death distills us into our two constituent parts, physiological and psychological. The physical side of us is obvious; it's the thing that we move around in, feed, try to keep in shape. Death's effects are most apparent there. The other part of us is the subjective experience of being "us", separate from our body. These are the higher-order thoughts, the consciousness, the neurological impulses that don't just keep our hearts beating and our lungs breathing; it's how we feel, what we think, what we decide to do. It's the part that produces objects, works of art, telephone bills, painful teenage poetry and Sunday dinner; it creates Facebook profiles; it connects with old friends across space and time. This is the mind, not the matter, and it's the part of us that's contested in debates about euthanasia, locked-in syndrome and what, ultimately, constitutes the end of life. It was in the Victorian era, as medical science made incredible discoveries about the physical body when we die, that psychology was established as a new discipline. Its objective was to describe the subjective experience of the mind. In tandem with our bodies, psychology believes, the mind forms who we are.

We are in a constant battle to keep our bodies, frail and mortal, functioning like well-oiled machines. Our cells would turn to mush if we lived forever. Our bodies are not built to survive. For this, medical research has provided intelligence ("the science bit"), but not solutions. As Colin Parkes, one of the world's leading psychiatrists in the field of bereavement, puts it, "Science may delay death but it can neither prevent it nor can it tell us anything about what, if anything, lies beyond death or what we can do to prepare for that transition." Our physical selves, ultimately, must die. It's our minds that want to live forever, that want to see, hear, taste, touch, smell, to form new memories, to produce new things, to meet the great-grandkids, to see world peace, but death affects that too: our minds, our psychologies also cease to be.

Even though all of that feels final, death isn't the end of us. It's only the denouement in the autobiographical "Story of Me". We may no longer be able to produce anything ourselves, unless you believe the spiritualists and others interested in the paranormal, but we continue on in the memories and imaginations of our survivors. We, or what people think of as "me", are still part of their lives, and what changes is who's in the driver's seat. When we shuffle off this mortal coil, we step down as the authors of ourselves – the uploaders of our photographs, the creators of our status updates – and continue only as shadows based on other people's memories and how they interpret what we've left behind.

Pre-internet, our post-mortem selves would have eventually faded out as the bits people remembered about us disappeared with their eventual deaths. But in the age of the web, we can continue to survive in more than physical objects that can be sold in garage sales or distributed amongst the bereaved. Thanks to the technology, we can now live forever, as Facebook memorial sites, Last.fm playlists, Twitter status updates, blogposts and homepages.

We, the living, dress up death in all kinds of ritual garb, and mourn our losses as if those who have departed are paying attention. Yet the ceremonies that orbit the body of the deceased, the bereaved and their community have emerged over time for very practical purposes. We clean the body because otherwise it would begin to rot and cause disease. Burying people six feet under means that decay is managed away from the local wildlife and from the living; the New Orleans adaptation of storing the dead in mausoleums arose because that city was built below sea level, and bodies had an unpleasant habit of rising risng from the earth whenever there was a storm surge. And in the UK, a small, populous country, it makes sense to reduce the physical part of the dead into the smallest footprint possible by cremating it.

Religious ceremonies too have evolved out of the bereaved's need to cope with their grief. Most religions specify the period of mourning (seven days of intense mourning in Judaism; 49 days in Buddhism; up to four months and ten days in Islam), the foods that should be brought to the family of the deceased (fruit in Hinduism; eggs and round objects in Judaism), and the forms of dress to indicate that the bereaved need special dispensation (black in most countries; white in Thailand; black and white in China). Most cultures also integrate offerings that will give the bereaved a feeling that they're helping the deceased on his or her way to whatever lies beyond.

"Each generation and each society has come up with its own solutions to the problem of death and has enshrined them in a complex web of beliefs and customs which, at first glance, seem so diverse as to be impossible to digest," Colin Murray Parkes and his colleagues explain in *Death and Bereavement Across Cultures*.

Technology is part of our modern world, so it's unsurprising that it has crept into our rituals. Digital anthropologist Genevieve Bell, director of interaction and experience research at computer firm Intel, says that technological culture has become part of Chinese funereal sacrifice: traditionally paper money was burned to help the deceased pay dues to cross into the afterlife; now paper iPhones, iPads and PCs are burned so they can be used in the other world.

Victorian society was obsessed with communicating with the dead; spiritualists adopted the new psychological scientific belief that the mind was separate from the body to explain the origins of bumps in the night. Our current relationship with death has changed monumentally since that time, mostly because of how we have medicalised disease and mechanised life. Because of what we now know about what's needed to keep our bodies alive, we are more likely to die in a hospital or other clinical setting than in the comfort of our own homes. Death has become a technical phenomenon, a medical condition, and has moved away from the centre of our communities to its periphery. In the West in particular, we're not encouraged to express ourselves through of grief, although, as Parkes puts it, such restraint is "highly deviant".

Despite the apparent differences across time and culture, these almost universal features of grief have found their way onto the web as well. In July 2005, I was living in Brighton, an hour south of London on the English Channel. I was beginning to cast around for the data that I would use for my PhD research, and I was collecting transcripts from the group discussions that were happening in the online virtual world Second Life. It operated a bit like a visual chat room: people were represented on the computer screen by characters, and they hung out and talked with other people who were also logged in at the same time. At the beginning, I didn't care much about what people were saying to one another, but rather who was talking with whom. I was interested in the web of relationships and how that was similar to or different from our offline networks. And then that all changed. The morning of 7 July was bright and the sea was choppy. The country was still buzzing from an eventful day before, when it was announced that London would host the 2012 Olympics. I was listening to the radio when news about the bombs on the London Underground and the number 30 bus came in. Within seconds, the country went from an epic high to a state of shock and horror, a low not seen since the death of Diana, Princess of Wales. I was working on my own at home and unable to get in touch with friends living and working in the capital because the phone lines were jammed. The TV was repeating the same information and I needed more. I needed to know about loved ones, but I had nowhere to go. So I went online. The official news sites were down, or only had the same information as the TV. Rumours were flying around the wires and there seemed to be nowhere to go. And then I remembered Second Life. There I joined what became a week-long period of public, but virtual, expression of grief. I collected hundreds of pages of the conversations people were having about the attacks, as they tried to make sense of what had happened and tried to cope with the tragedy, and what I discovered was that most of the things people were doing were identical to the ways that people try to make sense of grief and tragedy offline.

A virtual memorial became the focal point for many people's mourning. By 14 July, there was even a digital monument covered in virtual flowers, teddy bears, poems and photographs. People from all over the world left messages of comfort for anyone who had been directly or indirectly caught up in the attack, and shared their experiences if they happened to have been at the scene at the time. In the end, the London Memorial was visited by hundreds of thousands of account holders, with thousands of digital artefacts left behind for people to look at, click on and click through. This reminded me of the memorial that sprang up outside Kensington Palace in London after the death of Princess Diana. On both occasions, people were wracked by a very public grief that commentators couldn't make sense of, and in both contexts, people felt uncharacteristically free to display their confusion, horror and sadness.

Grieving is an essential part of healing. It rebuilds the scaffolding of life: the structures, the assumptions and the habits that formed part of the psychological attachment between the person who has gone and the people who are left behind. Coming to terms with the loss, and realising how you can move forward in life without that person, are only possible when the bereaved can accept how circumstances have changed. This is both inherently personal and very social. Public memorials serve as a focal point for people to express their grief and reorient themselves without their loved ones. Eulogies at funerals are often surprising, because most people don't know everything there is to know about the deceased. After their deaths we collect new stories about them from others who played different roles in their lives. Online shrines – dedicated websites or Facebook memorial pages, for example – are now an additional source of information, as people from across social circles come together in one virtual place to tell stories, share photos and find out more about the person who has died.

Our "culture of capture" means that many of our children are being recorded from birth through school and these records, warts and all, are uploaded to the network. The desire to collect memories is not new. We have been trying to record ourselves and our experiences for one another forever, whether through song, cave painting, poetry, photography or blogging. But as technology has developed, the cost of capturing everything with increasing accuracy has become almost negligible, from the stuff that might be considered significant to the socially rich, apparently pointless "phatic" communications (which is how Oxford researcher Danica Radovanovic describes the little details about what you had for breakfast or what the weather's like). Taken together, all of this digital stuff paints an extraordinarily detailed, intimate and almost lifelike representation of the person who is gone.

This can be disconcerting to those who are left behind. When I spoke to people about online memorials, many of them told of their surprise at the hubbub of activity on a loved one's profile, or the skeletons that fell out of an online closet. "It's a very weird thing, Facebook after death," said one interviewee who wanted to remain anonymous. "It's a strange, living memorial to which anyone can add and contribute – and which the family cannot control." The virtuality of the experience means that people who otherwise might not have been able or welcome to take part in the public grieving can now share. According to Tony Walter of the University of Bath, we are now sharing the experience of death in a way that we haven't for a long time. "Grief has become more public," he writes. And the connections that are forged within an online community that builds up around the death of someone – on a social network, or even in an online game – seem to last longer than those formed when strangers gather for a funeral offline.

Most social networks allow family members to access a deceased loved one's account, to turn it into a memorial page, to archive it or to delete it. Virtual memorials can be a source of comfort to those left behind. "Following the recent first anniversary of [my brother's] death," said the same commentator, "it was emotional, and not unpleasant, to log back on and see people posting anniversary messages and to see that he was still in the thoughts of so many people." The dead are becoming part of our society, and we're maintaining our connection with the deceased for longer. "There's a sense that online the dead are listening," Walter writes. And although this is a phenomenon that's been experienced by generations of bereaved people in cemeteries and séances, rather than having a private conversation between you and a headstone, when you write something on a dead person's wall, you are putting it out there, proudly, for everyone to see.

Many of us have, knowingly or not, merged our offline and our online lives. Things that pre-web might have featured in our last wills and testaments – real estate, stamp collections, cash and investments, cars, secret codes to prove there is life beyond the grave (allegedly left by escape artist Harry Houdini to his wife) or a gram of radium (from two-time Nobel laureate Marie Curie to her daughter) – are now only one part of our legacies. There is now a mass of digital information that we leave behind. John Romero started thinking about this in 2005, when his grandfather died. Romero, along with Evan Carroll, wrote the bible on the practicalities of death and dying in the age of the internet, *Your Digital Afterlife*. When Romero and his family were going through his grandfather's house, he discovered boxes of old photos and videos. "Six months later, my son was born," he says. "I was doing the new dad thing: taking [digital] pictures and shooting [digital] video. I'm thinking, there's nothing tangible about any of this, nothing to come out of a box in the closet in, hopefully, 60 years or so when I kick the bucket."

We saturate objects with a lot of psychological energy. They become reference points for who we are. This is why we treasure the things that loved ones leave behind after they die; they remind us of the people we knew. Uncle Bob's favourite tennis racket, Aunt Dana's antique coffee grinder, Emily's diary of her trip to Japan. They also remind us of who we are, because we knew those people. As we gravitate towards the web, however, the things we put online that are "us", like photos, videos, blogposts, homepages and status updates, are awkwardly ephemeral. They have no substance and we can't physically touch them, yet they're more permanent than our memories alone.

Still, intangible assets have a problematic way of disappearing. "A lot of people put their photos on [the photo-sharing site] Flickr and they don't keep them on their hard drive or anywhere else," says Romero. "These are valuable elements of your life that don't just have value to you but have value to other people as well." We won't necessarily be sad if the photos and videos of Romero's son that he's uploaded to Flickr or Facebook disappear, but for Romero's wife and son, they're part of their identities too. If they are deleted off a server because Romero's not around to pay the bill, his wife and son won't have access to them like they would to a box of old photographs. This is a new entanglement since the birth of the web. Unsurprisingly, at the same time we as a society progress through our lifespans while using technology to express who we are, we are beginning to figure out what's important to us and what isn't. And in response to this new knowledge, there's now a whole segment of the online industry that will help bereaved people hack into accounts of their deceased loved ones to keep the services updated – to keep those little identifiers alive. They'll also help you hack into other legacy things that have to be looked after when someone's died, such as bank accounts, bills, business emails, voter registration and other legal matters. These things require authority to access them, and if we don't put our usernames and passwords into a will or on a document in our office somewhere, this could cause problems. Increasingly, estate lawyers are recommending that people add digital assets to wills and trusts, including lists of online services with their associated usernames and passwords. Not only will this make it easier for your executors to tie up the loose ends of your estate, it will also help you to identify what you feel is part of you. You may decide that there are some things that you'd prefer to have die with you. After all, this is the final marker of your identity, your last chance to define who you feel you are. Plan ahead, advises Carroll in *Your Digital Afterlife*: "Take an inventory of the things that are important to you and make sure that the information needed to access those are passed on to a caring curator who will take over for you." Despite this, many executors aren't yet thinking about our digital assets, so find someone with the technological know-how to deal with your virtual life: "someone who has the authority and the technical understanding to take these actions for you."

What you have explicitly or accidentally chosen to leave behind remains only a slice of who you are. Machines are still unable to capture and replicate what it is that makes us human, either physically or mentally. Even in the current web age and with the unprecedented amount of computer power at our fingertips, we still only live on, just as before, as a collection of things and in other people's memories. But some people see a more interesting, if fantastical, future, where technology goes beyond preserving someone's identity for perpetuity in virtual memorials or building technologically-augmented gravestones. Those things are just collections of data that will, eventually, be written over or become obsolete. Some technologists are trying to use the processing power of the billions of computers that are hooked up to the network to create intelligences that could deliver the immortality that has been our obsession since we crawled from the prehistoric muck. People like Ray Kurtzweil and Vernor Vinge, authors, inventors and futurists, think that creating artificial life is not only possible but inevitable. They propose a cybernetic future in which we decant our memories into computerised systems so that we can upload them into fleshy bodies later, or even upload ourselves so that we can exist as consciousnesses in the network. They are two of the founders of the Singularity University in Palo Alto, California, where college courses are inspired by philosophy, academic research, religion, science fiction and (perhaps) the human's hubristic desire for immortality. I'll leave this cyborg future to the science fiction writers and the philosophers, who will use their skills to describe what being human is, and how we define death.

Would your thoughts and consciousness still be human, even if they existed only as a simulation in a vastly powerful computer some time in the future? This distinction between our physical selves and our mental states is a philosophical conundrum, but it signifies a line in the sand between those who believe our bodies make us human and those who define humanity by our thoughts and social lives. Such technology is currently impossible, but what the web shows us as it co-opts and adapts the rituals that we have used for centuries to help us transition between the living and the dead is that, even without a body, we do continue, in some new way, to be. Our real-life bodies may become obsolete, but online – unless the technology goes the way of the dodo – we cannot die.

"Your digital identity is going to be online when you are born, and it will follow you throughout your life," John Romero reminds us. "There will eventually be a marker that says that this person is no longer alive. That doesn't mean that identity should disappear, it's just that it should no longer be driving cars around or opening bank accounts or making credit card payments."

As we continue to live out our lives online, our virtual, non-physical actions will become even more important. The web has repositioned the dead in the centres of our worlds, forcing us to define ourselves by who we will be after we die. The way our deaths are entangled in the web is telling us more about who we are when we are alive than who we will be in the future.

LOSING MY MIND

What? What were you saying? I'm sorry. I was distracted: I was too busy trying to remember which of the 35 websites that I have open is the most important. My Blackberry inbox has 324 unread emails and Facebook has just popped up with a message saying someone wants to chat. I've got a message from Twitter that I have to look at, and my other phone just died, which means I have no idea what's in my schedule for the rest of the day. I've completely lost my train of thought. What were we talking about? Ah, yes: the web and its effects on our brains. Of course. Sorry. My apologies. You have my full attention. Do you have a charger?

It is the ultimate fear: that the machines are mucking with our minds. If I can't remember my phone number or what I needed from the shop, who I met at breakfast this morning and what we talked about, I blame the one thing that seems new and different in my life: the web. But this particular subject is the thing science actually knows the least about. According to Dr Vaughan Bell, a clinical neuropsychologist from University College London whose work has looked at the ways our brains go "wrong" and how they adapt to change, there have been very few studies that have tried to identify the relationship between people who use the web a lot versus people who don't use the web very often and their respective "attentional abilities". Despite the horror headlines and the fierce public debate, all we really have to go on about the neurological impact of the web is a feeling that our rapidly increasing use of technology in everyday life could be transforming us

from level-headed concentration kings into dumbed-down, quick-fix
click addicts.

Most of the other topics covered in this book, from privacy to
friendship to community, document the effects the web has had by
looking at the ways we were before and after we started going online,
but there are, literally, only a handful of research papers describing the
relationship between technology and brain function – from memory
to concentration and addiction – in the medical sciences. As such, I'm
afraid I can't make claims about its impact one way or the other. All I
can do is share what's out there. You'll have to make up your own mind.

One of the most famous examples of someone saying the web is
transforming us is in Nicholas Carr's web-dystopian polemic, *The
Shallows: What the Internet is Doing to Our Brains*. In it, he puts forward
a compelling argument that Google is making us dumber. He says it's
pandering to the lowest common denominator and giving us a quick
information fix. It doesn't challenge us to look anywhere else: with a
library of information at our fingertips so simple to navigate, we can
get answers to pub quiz questions without using our brains to recall
trivia, we can solve puzzles without making the connections ourselves,
and we can find out the meanings of words without moving from our
chairs, going to the shelf, finding the dictionary and looking them up.
The incredible service that made the web useful, the most successful
search engine in the world, is giving us exactly what we want, exactly
when we want it. Who needs to think critically when we get answers
to everything we've ever wanted to know on impulse, in an instant and
at the click of a button? This goes beyond Google, however. If we take
Carr's argument and run with it, our brains should eventually atrophy,
like a muscle that's never used. He says we're using our minds less

than ever before because it's so easy to find information. The web is a giant library of stuff that's so accessible, so "there". Like Augustus Gloop, storming through Willy Wonka's factory, grabbing everything he wanted and consuming it on contact, our brains are getting flabby: they're getting spoiled by abundance, poisoned by too much information and overwhelmed by too much stimulation.

Physiologist Baroness Susan Greenfield is an expert in neuroplasticity – how our brain cells, our neurons, adapt to stimulation. This is a hugely important part of human development. Because our neurons are naturally malleable, it means we can pick up language, we can adjust our behaviour, and we can evolve. It means we can learn. We make lots of new connections when we're kids, and we reinforce them as we get older. And what changes neurons is stimulation.

Baroness Greenfield believes the web is an instant gratification engine, reinforcing behaviours and neuronal connections that are making adults more childlike, and kids hungry for information presented in a super-simplistic way, that reduces their understanding of it to either "Yuck!" or "Wow!" There's no pause for thought any more, she argues. The way the web spoon-feeds us things to capture our attention means that we're learning to constantly seek out stuff that stimulates us. Our plastic minds are being rewarded by our quick-click behaviour: we want new interactive experiences, and we want them now.

The result, she argued at a 2010 all-party UK Parliamentary hearing under the heading "What is the potential impact of technology, such as computer gaming, on the brain?", is that kids are not developing an understanding of metaphor or abstract concepts. It's restricting imagination, she says, because short attention spans – a product of too much time playing games or poking friends on Facebook – means we now can't settle on anything for long enough to have an original

thought. Project this forward and in a dystopian digital future, we will
have no patience. We won't be able to concentrate. We will be childlike,
simple creatures. We will, literally, be doomed.

Baroness Greenfield's claims have never been adequately tested. In
fact, it's really difficult to demonstrate the effects of any media on our
cognitive capabilities or our behaviour, so statements about the effect
of "the internet" (as a single entity) on attention (also as a single entity)
are baseless. One of the reasons is that it's very difficult to identify what,
of all the things we are stimulated by, is having the supposed effect. We
live in a stimulation-rich world. When we log on, watch TV, read a book
or walk down the street, we are barraged by stuff. There are the things
that we can see, like TV shows, webpages or billboards, and the things
we can't see, like environmental and physical stimulants. Air quality,
sound, nutrition, social interactions, social norms, pheromones:
these are influences that are completely invisible but still affect our
brain chemistry. This is an incredibly interrelated and interconnected,
complex web of inputs, which makes it very difficult to separate out a
single effect on something as complicated as our minds.

A related problem with Baroness Greenfield's and Nicholas Carr's
claims is that they presuppose that once we use the web, that's it: we
are forever online. We will never log off again. Somehow we become
connected to our computers and other devices in a codependent,
exclusive, almost biological way, ignoring where, how and why we're
connecting. "Attention is a many faceted thing," says Dr Bell. There's
"sustained attention, divided attention, inhibition, spatial attention,
visual attention, auditory attention." He believes that if we want to say
anything of value about the impact of digital technology on our brains,
we have to look at what it is we're doing, and what kind of attention is
required. People do many things with digital technologies: "Someone

listening to GrooveShark while they paint the house is clearly not comparable to someone playing Unreal Tournament across the net," he argues.

We are still conscious when we go online that our interaction with the web is mediated by a device. We're affected by the device we're using, its keyboard or touchscreen, the sound in the room, the call from the kitchen that dinner is ready, the rumble of a phone in your pocket, the view of the outside rushing by the train window or the feeling of the seat you're sitting on, and we're also affected by the invisible stimulants in that situation. And beyond this, despite the increase in our use of digital technology, we still have to interact with one another face-to-face. We still have to use our bodies and minds to comprehend the world beyond the screen. The rest of the world doesn't fade away, and it still has an effect on our brains.

Despite this, the subject continues to be a low-hanging fruit for public debate, because all new technology – whether school books, newspapers, the telegraph, the railway or the web – causes anxiety, and every technological innovation introduces new behaviours that are pathologised by anxious people. "This has been the case for thousands of years, regardless of actual verified risks," says Dr Bell. These new behaviours that we're seeing as we use the web more and more do feel confusing. We keep 35 tabs open in our web browser. We flip between applications, games and websites constantly. We check our email when we're on the beach, we chat with friends on Facebook instead of going to the movies with them, and we spend our time playing online games instead of watching TV. Enter the pathologies: this may be why some people claim that digital technologies can be addictive.

The web has made it feel impossible not to be connected all the time, simply because it connects us. It feels as if the online world moves at speed, constantly transforming and redefining itself. Its very size and malleability reinforce the compulsion to participate lest we miss out on something that we want, and are compelled, to be part of. As our online lives increasingly integrate with our offline lives due in part to networks like Facebook, our social and professional reputations become tied in to our web connections. We have to feed and water these online relationships by responding to instant messages and tweets, by staying on top of the seemingly endless information at our fingertips, and by producing worthwhile online material. And there are only so many hours in the day ... Or so we tell ourselves. Really, it flatters our egos to believe we are indispensable. The rumble of a phone, a text message or an invite to an event makes us feel we're part of something. Unfortunately, the rewards are as difficult to predict as the weather, and it's this that keeps us obsessively checking in. Psychologist B.F. Skinner, father of cognitive behavioural therapy, described this "variable-interval schedule" in his 1950s behavioural model of classical conditioning: a response to a thing you do is reinforced randomly; there's no method to its madness, and so we create patterns of behaviour that try to either stimulate the thing happening, or respond to it as soon as it does. So, taking your email inbox as an example, the random reinforcement you get from a message landing in your inbox – enhanced by the expectation that it will, if you check it immediately after you wake up in the morning or come back into signal range – means that the outcome becomes more important than the process. Susan Maushart, author of *The Winter of Our Disconnect*, says, "We like to think that they are tools and we are the masters. If only life were that simple!"

The next digital literacy won't be about the nuts and bolts of how to use the web or a mobile phone, but how to set boundaries about when we let them encroach on our downtime. "Standing up to your

Blackberry is not standing up to the technology, it's standing up to your boss," says Douglas Rushkoff, media pundit and author of *Programme or Be Programmed*. In a move that's becoming increasingly popular among the hyper-connected, Maushart decided that she and her family needed a digital detox. She took everyone offline for six months. "My colleagues initially panicked, assuming that I was having a midlife crisis or maybe a good old-fashioned breakdown," she says. "But relationships remained intact – and most of the important ones not only did not deteriorate, but deepened." Sure, the web may make us feel more integrated, more productive and more wanted, but we do have to decide where the technology stops and our lives begin.

What's particularly interesting about the allegation that technology can be addictive is that addiction, whether alcoholism or problematic drug abuse or so-called Internet Use Disorder, changes neurochemistry. If Internet Use Disorder is in fact an addiction, it is a disease that requires medical treatment, support or therapy to get unhooked. At the moment, however, there's no evidence for the existence of Internet Use Disorder. None of the major medical or psychiatric associations have classified any form of internet use as addictive. In fact, they're very careful not to use the word "addiction", because there's no evidence that it is a unique disorder. All we have to go on, as the lay public, is that we see people use digital technologies in a different way to how we use media that we're used to and that have accepted behaviour patterns. Surely it's the way it's different that appears to be problematic? It could be problematic, yes, but rather than be something unique, it could simply be a symptom that uncovers another pathology: people who are treated for internet overuse usually have other problems as well. Compulsive use of the web may be a way to self-medicate an existing depression, poor impulse control or anxiety. Problematic overeating also falls into this pattern, as do other forms of compulsive behaviour.

The simple act of going online doesn't de facto lead to an admission to the clinic. Nor does a single drink lead to a trip to the Priory. Whatever the apparently unhealthy behaviour, there are some people who have predispositions towards compulsivity and addiction. It's not necessarily a genetic factor: research with identical twin pairs, in which one is an addict and the other is not, provides the evidence for this. Nor is it simple exposure. Psychologists have been trying to identify what causes some people to develop an addiction to something when another person doesn't become addicted to the same thing. Despite the absence of any official seal of approval from institutions like the American Psychiatric Association – the organisation that publishes the globally recognised *Diagnostic and Statistical Manual of Mental Disorders* – there are now web addiction clinics in the US, the UK, the Netherlands, China and South Korea. They take in the afflicted and wean them off their machines by reminding them that there's life beyond the screen.

The public conversations about our minds and the web tend to focus on the negative impact of technology, often ignoring the good things the web can do. Betsy Sparrow from Columbia University and her colleagues from Harvard and the University of Wisconsin believe it can free up headspace, leaving room for all kinds of new ideas. Memory is a fascinating thing. Generally when we think about it, we're mostly concerned with how quickly and easily it's recalled, not how it's stored. Cognitive psychologists describe many different kinds of recall triggers: episodic memory refers to information that you associate with a particular personal event, like a gig, a birthday or that sunny spring Saturday you took a cycle ride through the countryside with a couple of friends; procedural memory is what you use when you need to remember how to do things in sequence, like drive a car or write a letter – the things we generally don't think about once we've committed them into a routine; semantic memory is all about facts, faces and concepts. And there are other kinds of memory triggers, like emotional memories, memories we recall when we smell something, memories that we remember when we see another person.

When we come across a new piece of information, it's triaged through a system of complex pathways that, ultimately, lead to a brain bin of information we need for a long time, and one that we only need in the short term. We also cognitively stipulate if we need it all the time or infrequently. Sometimes the system is activated on purpose, like when someone asks us something and we pull up a relevant fact, and sometimes the system is activated accidentally, like when we recall a time when we were sad and are reminded to send flowers to mum or we lose ourselves in the smell of bacon and we remember a recipe we've been meaning to try.

Sometimes, we remember we have to remember something, and rather than keeping the information in our own minds, we pour that memory into another person, like a partner. So when we remember to remember, we go to that person who then reminds us when it's dad's birthday, or that we need to pay the phone bill. We also collectively share memories in social groups: one person might be good at remembering dates, while another might hold the memories for the names of everyone in the group. Another person may be an expert about who's vegetarian and who isn't. In these social groups, we collectively lean on each other to remember things. One of Betsy Sparrow's colleagues, Dr Daniel Wegner from Harvard University, calls this shared memory filing cabinet "transactive" memory. What it does to our brains is to lighten the cognitive load, allowing us to pay attention to other things. Rather than remembering the information yourself, all you as an individual in the group need to do is remember which person has the information you're looking for.

And this is what Sparrow, Wegner and their colleagues found is being transformed by the web: we are increasingly remembering fewer facts, like phone numbers, dates or where we had that fantastic burger in Central London last week, because we know where we can find them. On the web. We're beginning to treat Google like a member of our social group. Google remembers addresses, it knows where the person you need to get in touch with works, and possibly his phone number too, it knows who knows how to make pickled ginger; it can tell us who knows when Justin Bieber first cut his hair in that iconic style or where you can find out the locations of all of the remaining drive-in movie theatres in North America. Google has become the person who can read the road map. It's a good friend to have. Unfortunately, rather than using our newfound cognitive space to solve world hunger, we spend our time laughing at videos of cats instead.

Humanity has been using storage devices to hold on to things we need to pay attention to since we first painted a cave. Over time, we have become more dependent on our technologies. As we continue to tangle our lives up with the web, "the experience of losing our internet connection becomes more and more like losing a friend". Then again, recalling Dr Bell's warning, people said the same thing about the pencil. Most of the popular science debates that tackle the effects of technology on neuroscience can spin excellent yarns but, ultimately, their claims are based on a synthesis of hunches, agendas, supposition and anecdotal evidence. Still, it's the possibility of real physiological change that sells newspapers, books and tickets. We are told we can train our brains with computer games to become smarter, but we're also told that Google makes us stupid. Neither of these claims is true. When we believe pseudoscience that's dolled up as real research, all we're doing is unscientifically confirming our existing beliefs about what we think technology is doing to us. In this case, we think the web is making us more forgetful and more easily sidetracked. But, in reality, the technology is doing nothing to us; whatever it is that is happening, we are doing to ourselves. We can control the machine; it's not in charge of us. If you feel more distracted or if you think you're hooked on the web, take a step back. Turn off your smartphone. Close the lid of your laptop. Have a digital detox. Let your brain relax a little bit. Alternatively, let it be stimulated by the non-digital world: just as dynamic, as intense and as interactive as online.

Oh. Just one more thought before I go back to my open web browser, the Facebook chat, the Twitter message and the long list of emails that's landed in my inbox since I began writing this chapter: the web has only been around for two decades. Twenty years isn't nearly enough time to reverse millennia of evolution. It's way too early to really identify any long-term trends, good or bad. Don't throw the computer out of the window yet.

UNTANGLING US

In August 2003, at the height of the tourist season in New York, the east coast of the US experienced the worst blackout in its history, plunging a city known for its lights into total darkness. Over the next 16 hours, the people on the island of Manhattan were cloaked by a foreign and unsettling blackness, forced to bump into strangers who were somehow even more anonymous and unknown thanks to the trip of a very large switch. A lot of people were stranded and couldn't get home over the bridges or through the tunnels, while others couldn't get across town except on foot. And so hundreds of thousands of New Yorkers could do nothing but hit the mean streets, navigating around hawkers and through gridlock late into the night. The very dark night.

In a city like New York, already faceless, crowded and famously temperamental, these conditions could have flared up into disorder and chaos. Frankly, the city had a history: in the 1977 blackout, neighbourhoods were rocked by riots, looting and even death. Two years before, however, New Yorkers had discovered that they could rely on the kindness of strangers. As part of its coverage of the 2003 blackout, the *New York Times* described what transpired that evening as similar to what had happened two years earlier, during the aftermath of 9/11: "Mini-communities instantly formed near every car radio and boom box," wrote David Barstow the day after the lights came back on. A YouTube video posted by user drewdnyc shows New Yorkers helping one another, supporting one another, fanning one another in the heat, looking out for each other. Similar stories overwhelmed the social network Twitter during Hurricane Sandy in October 2012, when that storm blacked out a quarter of lower Manhattan for days.

Author Steven Johnson describes the web as a city, "built by many people, completely controlled by no one, intricately interconnected and yet functioning as many parts." If the Big Apple, known for its rough edges, can soften, and its anonymous citizens can reach out to protect one another, why do we expect that web communities – just as overpopulated and anonymous as any metropolis – can't also support social bonds in all their guises? In this section, I look more closely at this phenomenon, and describe how people coalesce online as they did in New York during the blackouts, in virtual groups that can be more powerful than their constituent parts.

In the early 2000s, while I was working on a television series about computer games, one of my co-presenters was given a copy of a "massively multiplayer" online game to review. Massively multiplayers are a genre of computer game where thousands of people log into the playing field at any one time and compete against or collaborate with one another. Two of the most popular are World of Warcraft and EverQuest. There are also enormously popular online strategy games, sports games and war games. The content isn't really important; the theory behind them is. When you're logged in, you can see everyone else wandering around, chatting, fighting, flying – whatever it is they have to do to complete their missions. It's a really odd phenomenon, and one that is uniquely web: these games are storytelling spaces where people have to work together with strangers and form groups in order to advance through the levels and win the ultimate prize. And, unlike other games, people play with people they've never met, who live in different towns, cities and countries, and who are collaboratively responsible for what happens in the story they're telling in the game world.

Far, far more interesting than any of the things they have to do to complete the game is what happens in between the formal "missions" that punctuate the game experience and drive the plot forward. It's rare for people to log off after finishing a mission. The virtual pubs (literally, in some cases) are full of post-match conversations, debriefs and general chat. People develop friendships during these downtime conversations, debating the play-by-play or just shooting the breeze.

They get to know how their game-playing buddies act under pressure. They figure out who's a team player and who isn't. They hang out just as they might do at the park or on the playing field. What happens online is weirdly like offline social life. There are community rules and regulations. People develop a strong sense of belonging that can influence what they do and what they think offline. There are cool groups and ones you don't want to be associated with. And these groups, these communities, are anything but short term. There are some groups of strangers who have known each other online for over twenty years.

According to the economists, lawyers, philosophers and developers who write the virtual worlds blog Terra Nova, there are social, political, governmental and legal systems that naturally occur when people get together online. Global governments keep an eye on these online communities to learn how to structure, design and implement social policies. They are social petri dishes. We can learn things from them, like how people form relationships and groups, why they form governments, who's at the top of the pecking order, and what happens when someone steps out of line. We can watch them to understand how groups flock around trends and fashions, and how they decide what is right and wrong. They give us a window into humanity in action rather than in made-up situations in labs or retrospectively after social systems have already settled into place. They are as-it-happens societies, even if they are mediated by machines.

It shouldn't be possible for communities to form online. A conservative definition of "community" always describes some kind of face-to-face interaction. But over the last century, sociologists have begun to observe different kinds of communities: those that are untethered from in-person contact. Sharing physical space is no longer a prerequisite for feelings of belonging.

Erving Goffman is a Canadian sociologist who spent his working life writing about what social and psychological functions communities serve, and how they affect the ways we think and behave. In his seminal handbook on the subject, *The Presentation of Self in Everyday Life*, which he published in 1959, he says they allow us to relax and to express who we feel we truly are. They give us a sense of belonging: we generate common symbols, shared stories, shared histories and shared languages. They provide safe places where we can play around with who we think we are, but where we know we'll be accepted and supported. And, he says, they can exist only in the heads of their members. All they need is a common purpose.

Online communities epitomise this: people gather around food, fashion, football, photography or ferrets. Whatever your interest, there's an online community for it. But now (as opposed to before the web), it's a lot easier for people to share interests and function like a community without having a physical basis for the relationship. In academese, they are "liberated communities of practice": conceptual spaces where people get together to share time and interests despite being in physically different worlds.

The problem with conceptual communities – the ones that aren't defined by in-person meetings and the exchange of physical goods – is that the absence of a tangible thing means they're difficult to measure and therefore to define objectively. Whereas a physical community has clear members, rituals and boundaries based on the things members do that can be seen and written down (like what kind of clothing they wear, or tattoos, or the colour of their hair), conceptual communities' activities are lost in the ether. This kind of philosophical messiness doesn't feel scientific, primarily because it can't be seen, touched, tasted or smelled. Communities that develop in places like beauty parlours, pubs and parks are easier to look at and say, "A-ha! These people are gathering here, therefore they are a community!" For some reason, it feels a lot less easy to say that about a web forum, a social network or a blog, which is why it's taken so long for people to truly accept virtual communities as social groups that are valuable to the individual and to society in general. When the first group of people went online, including a disproportionate number of anthropologists and sociologists, "it is probably fair to say that the emergence of community online was as much a surprise to online participants as it [was] to non-participants," says Professor Caroline Haythornthwaite from the University of British Columbia.

Still, these online places function as locations just like the beauty parlours, the pubs and the parks: they're neither home nor work. They give us a break from the expectations that saturate working and home life and they let us express who we feel we are based on our interests rather than our roles in those locations, even though they exist mostly in the minds of their members. They are "consensual hallucinations", in the words of author William Gibson: they live only in the eyes of their beholders. They are the hearts and the souls of our communities.

The real scaffolding of community, online or off, is something we can't see, can't touch, can't measure and can't put a monetary value on. Sociologists call it "social capital", a combination of the trust we have in our institutions and each other. It's like financial capital in that it has a value that can be used to trade, but the exchange is based on reputation rather than the gold standard, and the thing we gain is trust rather than a product or a service. Social capital gives us faith in one another, establishes our expectations and defines the rules of good behaviour. "It creates a society that is happy, well educated, healthy and safe," writes Harvard University's Robert Putnam. A community rich in social capital believes in volunteering, in looking out for one another, in caring for members of the community who are less able, in doing things that may not have immediate individual value, but ultimately allow the collective to thrive. Without social capital, our communities would fall apart: we wouldn't know who was reliable and who'd rob us blind. We'd lose our common language, our basic social structures would crumble, and even our economic systems would evaporate. Civil society would go up in smoke.

According to Putnam, this is the direction our societies have been going in for the last 100 years. Membership in organisations that he defines as "social capital rich", such as church groups and bowling leagues, Boy Scouts and political organisations, are dwindling, and local community, and indeed civil society, is suffering as a result. The culprit, according to Putnam, is technology: any technology that allows people to function collectively, but separately. So, looking back over the last century, mass uptake of the automobile connected people across towns and cities, but created suburban flight and urban sprawl; the national and international telephone networks let us bridge the distance created by the car, but distanced us even further from our core communities. And now the web has allowed us to live anywhere in the world and still feel part of a small town, but gives us a paper-thin sense of togetherness. "The internet is a powerful tool for the transmission of information among physically distant people," he wrote in 2000. "The tougher question is whether that flow of information itself fosters social capital and genuine community [...] Information itself needs a context to be meaningful."

*

Joi Ito is the head of the Media Lab, a powerful thinktank based at MIT, one of the most respected academic institutions in the US. The Media Lab has been one of the most influential research laboratories for developing cutting edge technology. It's also been in the pole position for describing human behaviour online. Before he took the helm at MIT, Ito was an eagle-eyed investor behind some of the world's biggest start-ups, including Twitter, photo-sharing site Flickr and music recommendation site Last.fm, and he belongs to a virtual community that's just as powerful as the Fortune 500 companies, or the Bildeberg Group. Ito and his virtual buddies are in charge of the modern world.

Less than a decade ago, he began playing World of Warcraft. Now, WOW may not be many people's idea of the kind of environment where high-flying CEOs and other business and government movers and shakers get together and broker deals, but this fantasy world – populated by flying monsters, spells and elves – is an important place in the networking landscape for people like Ito and his contemporaries. In his own words, "World of Warcraft is the new golf." Ito and others – "at least 10 have the letter 'C' in their job titles," reported technology site cNet in 2006 – formed a guild, or a group who spent their downtime working together (in virtual costume) to beat dungeon masters and other bad guys. They gave themselves a suitably conspiracy theory-inspired name, "WeKnow", and spent their downtime not on the fairway, but in the virtual country Azeroth collecting gold coins, drinking virtual mead, defeating enemies and discussing the relative merits of one virtual sword over another.

Researchers T.L. Taylor and Mikael Jakobsson have spent more than a decade watching these kinds of community groups form in online worlds like World of Warcraft, and describe what happens in these spaces in terms of what happens in offline groups like the Italian mafia: "[EverQuest, a popular online game] constitutes a primarily self-governed world in which complex social networks and systems of trust, reputation, insider/outsider distinctions, and alliances prevail. Who you know and your position within the larger social world is a central part of EQ gaming life," they wrote in 2003 in an article called "The Sopranos Meets EverQuest". Ito, himself no slouch, was rubbing shoulders with some of the most powerful business people in the world. We Know membership became as much a badge of honour as the college a person went to, or the frat house he belonged to. Some people even started including membership of We Know on their CVs. The bonds between Ito and the others in We Know were more than just information exchange: World of Warcraft provided the context that Putnam claimed the virtual world is without. And the social capital that was exchanged in the fictional country of Azeroth lasted long after Ito and his guild mates logged off.

Now, the ties that bind people together also gag. Our communities have a huge impact on what we think and what we do because our need to belong is strong. In 1951, psychologist Solomon Asch found that people will go along with a group if everyone else does, even if the direction they're heading is blatantly wrong. In his classic experiment, he showed a supposedly random group of people a line. He then showed them three more lines, only one of which was the same length as the original. The task for the group was to establish a consensus about which of lines 2, 3 or 4 was the same as number 1. As is typical in psychological experiments, only one of the people in the room wasn't in on the joke. The rest were confederates, told to pick the wrong line. The real test was whether the sole experimental subject would stick to his guns and pick the line that was obviously the right length, or go along with the crowd. The results were surprising. Overall, three-quarters of all of the experimental subjects – the people who didn't know what was going on – succumbed to peer pressure and chose the line they knew was wrong. They admitted as much to the people running the study afterwards. They made up all kinds of stories about why they did this: a common one was that they doubted their own perception. But they also made excuses for their decisions, saying they'd figured the rest of the group knew something they didn't, or that they knew the group's decision was wrong but they didn't want to draw attention to themselves. Whatever the reason, Asch's famous study showed that in many instances we will conform to a majority even if we know it's wrong. Why? Because it's lonely being on your own.

The experiment was later modified to pick apart its subtleties. One of the ways it was adapted was to split the confederates into several groups. One group of people who gave an incorrect answer had the same gender as the experimental subject. Another group shared the same skin colour. Another was a totally fabricated identity: they'd been placed into either the red group or the blue group. These were enough to get him or her to conform to that group's response, even if it was clearly wrong.

We conform to what psychologists call a social identity: a community that we think we belong to more than another one. Our social identity is that bit of our psychological makeup that belongs to larger social structures: female, American, psychologist, volleyball player. Social identities are the classic conceptual communities. You can join the Women's Institute, wave a flag, become a paid-up member of a society or be part of a team, or you can just believe in your mind that you are these things. What goes on in your head still has an impact. We don't want to be excluded by people who we think are like us, and that's why we will give in to group pressure, even if we think that the group is wrong. So how do we know what the people in our conceptual communities think? We have two strategies: we ask, or we make it up.

When you see status updates from people on Twitter or on Facebook asking things like, "How do we feel about X?", where X is a new product, a comment, a music video, a political speech or an opinion, you're witnessing community boundary negotiation and identity definition at its most obvious. But the reason it exists, and so blatantly, is because we have so little to go on online. Our online conceptual communities are based on a lot of assumptions; we fill in a lot more blanks than we would offline, and so the definition of what's acceptable or not can be a little unclear.

All we have in order to judge how similar we are to a stranger in our online community is what they say and do. Offline, we can decide if we're like or unlike someone else based on non-verbal cues like the clothes they wear, or the colour of their skin, or verbal indicators of similarity like their accents. All we really know about someone else in an online community is that they like the same kind of music we do, or share the same political opinions, or are also fans of our favourite movie. Online, we're more likely to follow the crowd because of a peer pressure that more than likely doesn't exist. This doesn't mean that our online activities are turning us into a society of sheep, willingly and blindly following the flock in whichever direction it takes us. There are still people whose opinions we rate more than others. We create in our heads a caricature of a person who we think represents that group: a prototype, something we can compare ourselves with. This prototype represents a group member that is the most feminine, the most American, the ultimate psychologist, the ultimate volleyball player. It might be based on someone who's real or it could be a pastiche of several people we'd consider good reference material. Where this conceptual prototype comes from doesn't matter: we decide if we want to be like this figure in our heads, and based on what we think they might think, we then guess how they might respond to new product X or political opinion Y.

Most online communities that support social capital have pecking orders and people who are prototypical often are at the top. This is why people who want to sell us things are increasingly targeting people high up in online communities. They're exploiting their virtual social capital – their ability to get information out in the right context. When a friend or someone we respect announces that she likes something on Facebook, or tweets a link, we are more likely to take a look because we think it's more valid than a message from a stranger. Online campaigns spearheaded by respected bloggers can take down legislation. And if a celebrity endorses a product or service, they can easily crash a website within minutes. "Opinion leader convergence strategies" convince entire networks of people that not getting on board carries social rejection, a worse social consequence than giving in.

Facebook's "like" button is probably one of the most important innovations in the modern social influence toolkit. For little to no effort, I can give a thumbs-up to a product, a charity, a YouTube video or a news article, and this information is instantly beamed to the right people in the right social context. What do I get? Well, apart from flexing my thumb for a particular online community, I raise my value within my social group. Everybody wins: the circle is complete. Clever move, Mark Zuckerberg. But there's more: the publicness of the "like" action not only gets the message out to a much broader audience than traditional means would, but is also more likely to convert people to a cause. The more friends you see who "like" a thing, the more it becomes part of your community's identity, not just your own. More people within the group will bow to social pressure and "like" the thing themselves, demonstrating that they are also part of that group by wearing it as a badge of honour. Eventually, it will achieve critical mass and a movement will be born.

This can have a real-world effect: virtual communities naturally complement their offline counterparts, and some of the most influential movements in the last decade – from political changes in northern Africa to social and economic changes in developing nations such as India – have been a result of a clever combination of online and offline campaigning. These techniques manipulate the sense of togetherness that we get from being part of a community and the way we can connect across borders with people who share our social identities. It's a powerful combination of human psychology and media manipulation.

Those are the communities we choose, the ones we're aware of. But we're also lumped into other communities by marketers and, increasingly, by software. Amazon tells us what we might like based on which tribe it thinks we're part of. Google tells us information in the same way. These services make their livings by suggesting things that people like us have liked. And how do they know who's like us? By putting us into communities based on what we do online.

Your computer-determined community is based on a couple of things. First, what you tell the system directly. If you have a social network profile, you tell it your name, age, gender, religion, relationship status, favourite music, where you work, where you're from, which networks you belong to. So far, so offline. But these are very simple descriptions, and don't capture the whole you. They don't describe which book you'd take to a desert island, why you hate your boss, or why you think about your grandmother when you smell freshly-baked chocolate chip cookies. They can capture bits of you, but the stuff that's hard to pin down can't really be put into a database. Writer Jaron Lanier describes what we're doing to our identities when we fill in the forms about ourselves on social networks as "self-reductionism": the boxes that we tick in our Facebook profiles construct us, for the purposes of their database, as a collection of keywords.

Second, your computer-determined community is based on the cloud of information that a service has collected about you based on what you've done online. Little pieces of code, called cookies, live on your web browser and tell a service like Facebook, Google or Amazon where you go and what you look at. That trail of information becomes the online version of you. It is, however, a one-size-fits-all solution. The database is permanent, and it assumes you'll be the same forever. It doesn't understand how much we change throughout our lifespans or capture the contradictions that come out in different ways for different people in different contexts. I may have clicked on the film *Robin Hood: Prince of Thieves* more than any other movie in iTunes, but that doesn't make it my favourite, or the most influential film in my life. I may have voted for the Left in the last election, but that doesn't mean I won't vote for the Right next time around. I may have really liked The Monkees when I was 12, but that doesn't mean I still like them at the age of 37. Who we are changes throughout our lives, and different groups become more or less important to us too. We're not a single, fixed person from cradle to grave, but the ways the technologies currently work and the ways they're being used to get us to pay attention and be influenced by something don't take this into consideration. These are the filters through which we see the online world. Sure, we can make friends and find people, but now there are other people watching and categorising us, manipulating our social lives for their purposes.

The effect is that our seemingly random pathways through the web are actually determined by what we want to know and what we want to hear. The commercial services that dominate the digital world – the Googles and the Facebooks – are trying to keep us brand-loyal by delivering services that meet our needs, so they confirm our biases by telling us things that we already want to hear.

What happens when it's not just products that we're interested in, but greater, global issues?

Lada Adamic at the University of Michigan was one of the first to expose this echo chamber in online political discussions, showing that Democratic blogs linked to Democratic blogs and Republican blogs linked to Republican blogs in the 2004 US presidential election. We're becoming less interested in different ideas, foreign news and opinions that clash with our own. The vast ocean of information online is increasingly navigated by packs of like-minded people who really only see a little slice of what is available on the web.

But we can't blame the technology completely. Putnam reminded us in 2000 that birds of a feather flock together. It is because we are drawn to communities of people we believe we are similar to and both like and want to be with that technologies have been developed to exploit this. In social media, we will clump together just like the neighbours with their air conditioning units and the farmers with their corn seed.

"Community" has forever been under threat. In recent history, the culprits were believed to be from industrialisation and urbanisation, and later technology. The truth, however, is that most of us aren't living in pastoral villages any more. We have migrated to the big, faceless city, where crime is on the rise and our quality of life is in decline. We can't blame the web for these changes: "Each new disruption in the (imagined) ideals of home and town is met with resistance and fear of the further degradation of our daily experiences," says Caroline Haythornthwaite, who's been a close observer of the interplay between online and offline life for more than a decade. The benefits of community, whether online or off, become apparent if you focus on how people connect and what they get out of their communications.

Personal relevance is what drives what we are influenced by. We live under comfortable duvets of information that confirm our beliefs, determined by language, culture and interests. The technology is not doing anything to us; it is responding to our human psychological instinct to belong.

Difference is inspiring, catalysing and progressive. Social psychological research over six decades has found that inward-looking groups, online or off, will have less tolerance for the other. They're more antagonistic, confrontational and bigoted. In other words, because of the way the web helps us form strong online communities – the like-mindedness, the friendships, the social capital – and because of the way the technology encourages this by filtering out difference, the way we currently navigate the online world may result in social division instead of social cohesion. Thankfully, we are not automata. We shape the technology to fulfil our needs, not the other way around. We still exist in a world away from the computer, and we will continue to do so. We are exposed to a variety of conflicting viewpoints in everyday life, as we traverse school, work and play. If the online world was all we had I'd be worried. But it's not. We still have our offline communities and human variations. If we're aware of the dangers, we can stop this trend towards balkanisation, and reach out and touch someone new.

UNTANGLING THE BEDSHEETS

I would describe my sexual activity as pretty vanilla. There was a time when it was perhaps more rocky road, but I've since settled into a beneath-the-bedsheets (or otherwise) grind that's no more and no less extreme than most. I've found a form of sexual expression that I like and I am comfortable that it represents who I feel I (currently) am and who I want to be.

That doesn't mean I'm not fascinated by other people's kinks. Most of us are. All you need to do to confirm that we are bonkers about the ways other people bonk is to look at sales figures for saucy novels like *Fifty Shades of Grey* or *Lady Chatterley's Lover*. Or how quickly the news of footballer Ryan Giggs' indiscretions ricocheted around Twitter, despite a superinjunction that was supposed to keep them under cover. Or, indeed, at the extraordinary $14 million that Escom LLC paid for the domain name "sex.com" in 2006.

Now, I generally have a very open mind about what people get up to. A friend of mine was the editor of a fetish mag for several years in the mid-1990s and her bookshelves are stuffed with books and 'zines – glossy photo essays, academic deconstructions, photocopied illustrations and Haynes-style how-to manuals – about everything from the familiar "alternatives" to the downright eyebrow-raising. I can get lost in Ruth's stacks for days, so imagine what the apparently bottomless pit of the internet offers someone like me.

A caveat: my interest in this subject is in consensual sex online, not the plenty on the web that trades in exploitation and horror, which is expertly covered by writers like Brooke Magnanti and Laura Agustín. Here, I'm curious about what effect the bounty of virtual booty has on our offline selves and society, as the moral panic about unregulated self-expression reaches a fever pitch.

The web is generally considered a problem when it comes to our intimate activities: words like "ubiquitous", "hardcore" and "uncontrollable" often crop up in the press, fanning the flames of fear. The research doesn't help: most of it tries to unpick the relationship between cybersex addiction and criminal behaviour, framing sexual activity as a problem from the outset. But is it? The web is a gathering place and a facilitator for all kinds of attitudes and behaviours, not just the sexy ones. But sexual subcultures exist. They always have, with or without communication technology. And so the web is, effectively, a magnifying glass, scrutinising the depth and breadth of our most intimate behaviours. There really is nowhere to hide.

Online sexual content varies wildly. There are sex education and self-help forums that are eye-wateringly graphic, animated games that brim with pornographic imagery and language, sites for communities with very specific kinks (not least Kink.com, founded in 1997 by PhD student Peter Acworth), hugely popular video sharing sites like YouPorn, and virtual havens where consenting adults can have interactive cybersex. There are as many online communities as there are subcultures, and places to meet, greet and try before you buy, so browsers can find the sexual expression that's right for them. The "sex positive" movement, promoted by columnist and podcaster Dan Savage, is responsible for encouraging the "tech savvy at-risk youth" to find personal fulfilment and, as he says so often in his Savage Love podcast, to make sure that the things done in the bedroom – no matter how far out – don't leave people or their partners curled up in foetal positions, weeping in the corner of the room.

"Sex is the area of human experience that embraces the vastest range of possibilities," says Cindy Gallop, creator of the sex education website MakeLoveNotPorn.com. Cindy's site epitomises the web's disruptive possibilities. British-born New York resident Cindy, in her fifties, is open to the point of boastfulness about her interest in men in their early twenties. And thanks to a voracious consumption of sexual partners of that age, she claims to have first-hand experience of a shift towards the extremes, as more of this group are exposed to online (and offline) porn. Cindy, as an experienced lovemaker, gently explains to her partners that their behaviours under the bedsheets aren't, perhaps, appropriate for everyone. But she realises that she's preaching to a small gene pool, and that to inspire a real change in sexual behaviour, she needs to talk to another audience. MakeLoveNotPorn.com is Cindy's way of saying to young women that what happens in porn (in general) isn't what making love is all about. Women don't experience explosive orgasms every time they're touched, for example. There's no need for multiple penetration in sexual encounters. Anal sex isn't the norm.

Cindy and her contemporaries are emphatic that discussions about porn generally lead to an interpretation about what's sexually good and bad, usually framed around a monogamous, heterosexual experience. Instead, they say, there's room for all kinds of porn that's left out of the discussion. And our access to cheap recording technology and a global distribution platform like the internet means that the vastest range of possibilities is out there for human consumption.

According to Sai Gaddam and Ogi Ogas's book *A Billion Wicked Thoughts: What the World's Largest Experiment Reveals About Human*

Desire, the US content filter "CYBERsitter" blocked 2.5 million adult content websites in 2011. This may seem a lot, but with over a trillion sites created since its beginning (according to web guru Kevin Kelly in his book *What Technology Wants*), adult content doesn't actually constitute a huge proportion of online life. Regardless, our uncomfortable relationship with sex means we're awfully concerned about what those sites are doing to us.

Now is not the first time technology has been accused of changing society's ideas about sex. "Put new technology and sex together and it seems you'll always get waves," begins EroTICs, a report about sexuality, the internet and women from the California-based Association for Progressive Communications. "Victorian societies were scandalised by the arrival of the telephone because women – who were chaperoned at all times – could potentially talk with suitors in private." Sex, technology and social politics have always been intimately entangled. The reason the web challenges the received narratives is because the stories people can and do tell one another can no longer be under anyone else's control. And for some reason, we assume the worst.

"Older media are dominated by a view of sex as scandalous and dangerous, and their depiction of sex has been pretty predictable," says Professor Feona Attwood of Sheffield Hallam University. Attwood is the editor of Porn.com, a collection of research from the leading specialists in this field. She believes that online sex is not per se a problem for human sexuality, or even necessarily a game-changer for society. But we tend to hear about it when it does become a problem. It's not just the fault of the mainstream media – most of the research about online sex comes from clinical settings like therapy practices or hospitals, rather than looking at its effects on "normal" populations.

It's therefore not surprising that reports focus on addiction, offences and relationship problems.

What is the reality? Sex addiction is recognised by the psychiatrist's diagnostic bible, the *Diagnostic and Statistical Manual of Mental Disorders*, or *DSM-IV*. It's characterised by a compulsive need, usually by men, to have sex or look at sexual material so much that it harms the sufferer, or the people around him or her. But if you are concerned that stumbling onto a porn site will transform you into an online sex addict, the research says that unless you already have a problem with sexual compulsivity or are psychologically vulnerable, it is unlikely to become an issue. Given that 80.5% of the 400 heterosexual men studied by Stanford University psychologist Al Cooper in 2004 said they looked at some kind of online sexual content to distract themselves or to take a break, this is good news. And this also has to be a relief for parents who are worried about what happens when their children are exposed to sexual content on the web. For kids, sex is compelling, arousing and, frankly, rather confusing. They're trying to figure out who they are as they perform a complex and often uncomfortable dance around their emerging interests and what they think everyone else like them should be like. This includes the development of a psychosexual self. In the online playground, they can seek it out, stumble upon it, talk about it and showcase their interests, just as they always have done in the offline playground, the library and behind the bike shed. The difference is, of course, that they can do it anonymously and with less potential financial or social cost.

Grownups have access to their own online playground, and a lot of the discouraging popular discourse is worried about the effects of adults' porn consumption on kids. In 2006, Jill Manning looked at the impact of internet porn on marriage and the family, and yes, being exposed to porn does have an effect on kids. Just like the offline version – as well as cultural shifts in the media, the commercialisation of sex and the role of the pharmaceutical industry in altering public views on sexuality and sex – online sexual content has been associated with earlier sexual activity and less-than-vanilla pursuits. But kids are naturally critical about what they see. Most often they report being shocked, disgusted, embarrassed, angry, afraid and sad. With a supportive emotional base, kids are critical of sexual content online and off, but this requires a healthy attitude to sex in the first place.

There is another side to online sex that's rarely reported in the papers: the positive side.

"The dominant discourse on sexuality and the internet is, more than often, framed around 'dangers'," says Karen Higgs of the Association for Progressive Communications. This concern may be misplaced, judging by the interviews she conducted for the EroTICs research report. Rather than focusing on the web's downsides, many of the people interviewed described it as a place to learn about their sexual rights. Thanks to the anonymity and accessibility of the web, sexual support groups and sex education sites have exploded in number and popularity. People need no longer get over their embarrassment to ask someone whether they're broken or wrong: they can go online and find out from professionals or other people who are suffering the same conditions or concerns. There are problems with this (explored in greater detail later in this book), but when it comes to the development of a healthy psychosexual identity, the web is an unparalleled innovation. In a digital world, we all have access to a printing press and an audience. "The web permits you to write your own stories, describe your situation, inhabit another character, expand on exciting stories, detail your sexual life through blogging or create your own," says Dr Petra Boynton, a sex educator at University College London, with more than a decade of experience as an online agony aunt. This has created a treasure trove for an audience that's made up of more than the heterosexual, male-oriented point of view that's primarily represented in old media sexual content.

"You'll find many of the same things online as you will in other media," says Professor Attwood (from the research collective, Porn. com), "but what's also out there are amateur scenes in domestic settings: queer, kinky and feminist pornographies; subcultural and indie productions; lots of erotic and pornographic storytelling; practices which mix the sexual display we associate with porn with dating or social networking." Women in particular are able to find and generate images, videos, stories and scenarios that they feel represent who they are more accurately than non-web porn. "The most striking thing, for me, is the way porn has become accessible to women," explains Professor Attwood. "Earlier forms of porn distribution, which relied on visits to sex shops or being passed among men, made it really difficult to get hold of. The web has made it possible for women to access porn easily, which is important for the way it will develop."

"Old media porn is a one-size-fits-all solution," says Boynton. New media porn, Boynton, Attwood and the sex positive proponents argue, is a solution for sexual enlightenment. And this really shakes things up, particularly under the bedsheets.

What Dr Boynton, Professor Attwood and their fellow practitioners have found is that access to sexual material on the web has not changed the essentials of how people develop their sexual identity. Men, gay or straight, still come to Boynton with concerns about their anatomies; women continue to be worried about body image, relationships and pleasing a partner. The main difference between the pre-web teen magazine problem pages and the post-web emails Boynton and Savage now receive is the vocabulary: "The questions are more explicit – asking about oral or anal sex, or sexual techniques." This kind of language may shock parents, but Boynton thinks the explicitness is a good thing. "We now have a much broader lexicon to identify what it is that we're into," she says, and can therefore get to the nitty-gritty of any problems more quickly. But the graphic nature of the language people now use to describe what goes on in the bedroom can come as a surprise to people who are confronted by it when they don't expect it.

Those on the front line also spend time dealing with questions about infidelity and, yes, technology can make it easier to do things that might lead to the breakdown of relationships. Mobile phones and other portable web-enabled devices allow for unobserved interactions, online porn is only a click away and dating sites offer the opportunity for discreet encounters with new partners. The web provides plenty of hidden nooks where someone searching for a bit on the side can share an intimate moment with a friend or stranger.

There is no evidence, however, that the technology causes people to play around. Most couples counsellors report that there's most likely already a problem in a relationship before people start fooling around offline or on. The intimacy that people experience online can make a relationship that's having problems even more unstable. But are online indiscretions really the same as an offline love affair?

The web is a communication technology that introduces a novel computer-facilitated intimacy. Monica Whitty at the University of Leicester has been studying the psychology of online romance since 2002, and her work has been important in defining the emotional aspects of relationships in the digital age. "The online relationship is considered to be as real as the offline relationship," she wrote in 2005. So it's not surprising that online infidelity – including looking at internet porn – seems as "authentic and real as offline acts".

The brain is an incredibly powerful erogenous zone. The research about arousal and fantasy is extensive, and includes everything from gender differences in fantasy content to what happens to arousal when a brain injury affects the ability to fantasise. There are academic journals dedicated to it, not to mention commercial industries. The web allows people to interact in real time in unprecedented ways. Put the brain and the web together and the possibilities are explosive.

Couples counsellors and psychologists who study love say that sex is a necessary part of a healthy long-term relationship. Although many couples who don't experience physical intimacy can still have a good relationship, sex can serve as an emotional adhesive. Particularly in the early stages of a love affair, sexual desire is a reciprocal exchange that cements bonds and, without it, a partner might begin to wonder what role he or she plays in the other person's life. Most people think this kind of intimacy isn't possible if a computer is in between lovers, but what if two people are separated by distance – maybe they met online and live in different places, or maybe their lives and jobs keep them apart? "Couples in long-distance relationships naturally turn to technology," write Saul Greenberg of the University of Calgary and Carman Neustaedter of Simon Fraser University. The pair have studied how people keep relationships alive even when they can't physically be together. A common technique is leaving video chat on while making dinner or doing the dishes. You get the sense of having your lover in the same room, but you don't necessarily need to give him or her your total attention, as you would during a phone call. This kind of technologically mediated intimacy plays an important part in maintaining a sense of closeness, but what about when the couple are feeling frisky? The most common form of play between long-distance couples is via video link but, according to Greenberg and Neustaedter, most couples don't feel it quite hits the mark.

For more adventurous types, the web offers other opportunities. Kyle Machulis is an engineer who works for a robotics company. By day, he builds cars that drive themselves. By night, he is qDot, the blogger behind open-source sex technology site Slashdong. He is the world's leading expert in web-based adult toys. "Teledildonics are mechanical sex toys that are driven and controlled by a computer over a network," Machulis explains. "You have an interface on your computer that'll be able to control speed or movement of someone else's hardware, and they'll be on the other end of the network being able to use the toy you're controlling." Of course, this isn't everyone's thing. "A lot of people are scared of their computers," he admits. "Chances are that if you're scared of installing your printer, you really don't want to be intimate with it either." But, because of these devices, it is possible to be more or less physically intimate with someone you love, to the extent that there is both a real-time interaction and a feeling that your partner is present or at least involved. "Usually the most successful toys, no matter what kind of interaction or control they use, are those that hook you up to another person," Machulis says, explaining that solo play with artificially intelligent computers does exist but is a minority sport. The most successful experiences, he maintains, are between long-distance partners. "You have the ability to be intimate just using the network. It's augmented just like phone sex, but you're adding a couple more elements that make it a little bit more intimate."

For those who are less inclined to engage in cybersex but still want the feeling of intimacy that comes with being in the same room as a long-term lover, there is a growing number of apps that will provide this. "Haptic" or "affective" technologies use the network to communicate non-verbal intimacies like a gentle touch or a heartbeat. "It's certainly not going to replace physical, actual, real-contact intimacy at any point soon, if ever," Machulis says. "Our brains are really just not wired that way." But in a kind of postmodern way, these technologies can help us to maintain the emotional bonds that are at the heart of a healthy relationship.

Most people are at least intellectually familiar with the idea that the internet is kinky, whether it is because they are involved in it themselves, or they have stumbled across an article or television show claiming that the new technology corrupts society by exposing us to unheard-of sexual practices involving harnesses and balloons. (Of course, these exposés are usually accompanied by detailed descriptions, photos or videos of the harnesses and balloons.) Our response as a society shows not just our discomfort with sex but also our prejudices about who has a right to express sexuality and what kind of sex practices are OK.

When I moved to the UK from the US in 1994, one of the first major culture shocks I experienced was that the newspaper with the highest circulation in the country prominently featured a photo of a topless woman on page three. When I said something about it, I was firmly reminded that the US was the one corrupting youth because of its hardcore porn industry. I still don't get this particular localised cultural expression, but there are other, more generalised sexual norms that I don't see the logic in either, like the outing and vilification of female sex bloggers. "There's an idea about how women express sex and sexuality," says journalist Zoe Margolis, the sex blogger exposed by a UK national newspaper as The Girl With The One-Track Mind. Margolis' popular blog, detailing her sexual encounters under the nom de plume Abby Lee, had won over 250,000 readers until she was outed by *The Sunday Times* in 2008. After losing her anonymity, Margolis also lost her job in the film industry and disappeared from public view before returning to express her side of the story in competing newspapers. In conversation, she's described the way women are unable to talk publicly about sex as "a real double-standard", a viewpoint shared by Boynton, who describes public criticism of sexual content on women's websites in particular as "an exercise in 'slut shaming'." Although the web does offer an outlet for sexual expression for all, there are still limits to what is considered acceptable that are imposed by the rules of wherever (and whenever) it's consumed, and the global publishing platform makes those cultural differences more obvious than ever before.

There have been situations in which images used for educational purposes have been mistaken for porn. For example, health advice about breast cancer has been blacklisted because the word "breast" raises red flags. There are other cases where something from the past can re-emerge and reignite problems in the modern era. In one notable case, an image of rock group Scorpions' 1976 album was decreed child pornography by the UK Internet Watch Foundation, which caused a lockdown of the Wikipedia site.

There is no one solution for regulating online sexual content. Different governments take different approaches: some, like the UK and France, prefer "lightest touch", aiming towards a system of self-regulation at the internet service provider level, while others are trying to institute national firewalls. A top-down solution for regulating sexual content online for whatever reason – child protection, social control, retaining the status quo – is impossible to implement, because it would never be flexible enough to adapt to our ever-changing, constantly fluctuating norms regarding sex. And, frankly, it's easy for people with knowhow to get around filtering systems.

Shutting down the potential for creative expression and inter-personal intimacy would undermine the basic tenet of the web. It's therefore unsurprising that we must face how we as a global society cope with our social and cultural differences, when one of the most emotionally charged elements of humanity rubs up against the free expression inherent in the network.

We have historically been weaned on a heterosexual, monogamous and male-oriented approach to sex. Everything, from media to mental health manuals, from faith to family values, has preached this point of view. Even our politicians have been the arbiters of sexual propriety. Of course, as they have demonstrated, there are many, many variations to this norm. People want fulfilment, and they will seek it out. Discovering our sexual selves is part of our psychological development. How much we can perform this, though, this depends on the tools we have to express ourselves and the acceptance of a like-minded and supportive community.

Now, thanks to the web, Pandora's box has been opened. We are stripped bare, exposed and forced to confront who and what we are: kinky, curious and made up of many shades of grey.

WHERE HAVE ALL THE KIDS GONE?

In June 2012, Facebook announced that it would throw its virtual doors open to a whole new population. Since it was launched to the general public in 2006, two years after it was set up by its CEO Mark Zuckerberg as a dating portal for college students, the site required all users to be over 13 years old. That age restriction protected them from all kinds of potential lawsuits and, after all, there were plenty of other social networks catering to the tween set: Club Penguin, Moshi Monsters, cBeebies, Bebo, Cyworld, Habbo Hotel. Plenty. Why would the kids need to come to our playground? Well, it turns out that kids were already there. In 2011, an extensive survey of 25,000 children and their parents across 25 countries reported that almost 40% of 9–12-year-olds already had profiles on the site. The report, called EU Kids Online, led by Professor Sonia Livingstone and her team at the London School of Economics, found that one third of the underage Facebookers had lied about their ages to get in. The rest of the 10,000 kids who confessed to being on the social network said a family member or friends had signed them up. So much for the age policy. But surely this didn't come as a surprise. Kids have grown up with the web and, as far as they're concerned, everyone has a Facebook account. For many people, Facebook *is* the web. To go online is to go on Facebook. Older kids talk about what they do there; you see it on your favourite TV shows; some of your friends might even be there. Of course you're going to try to get in, duh. And getting in is really not that hard to do.

Given that Facebook was already peppered with children who had networks of friends, who were joining groups, who were organising events and who were sharing photos and phone numbers, what could it do? One option was that the company could create a kids-only version. The company would be able to police it with an iron fist, making sure to keep the wrong people out. The problem is, they'd have to make it compelling enough to keep the right people in, and no grownup online community has ever managed to spin off a successful underage clone because, from the kids' perspective, the action happens where everyone else is. And what happens when they hit the golden age and can graduate upwards? They'll have to leave their younger friends behind. If a social network is built to connect you and your mates, you want to be there. Commercially, companies risk alienating their customers by segregating the kids from the grownups, and something else will come along that will let them all play together – somewhere that's neither of your sites, and where you can't make any money.

From a parent's perspective, a child's version of Facebook may initially appear safer because it's like having a permanently staffed online crèche, but many of the parents that Professor Livingstone and her colleagues interviewed said that they'd signed their kids up to the 13+ version so they could keen an eye on them. Being aged over 13 themselves, they wouldn't be able to track their offsprings's behaviour in an under-13s site. They'd have to trust the system.

The other alternative was that Facebook could let the kids into the regular version and make their underage users safer. And this is exactly what they did. Technologically, if a kid registers their actual age rather than a fabricated, inflated 13+ age just to get in the door, the system can identify them and assign certain features to their accounts that would make their Facebook experience more secure. They could restrict other people's access to their profiles, making them invisible to the rest of the network, or only allow selected friends to chat or share content with. As a bonus, the kids would develop a brand loyalty to Facebook Inc., and would stick around through their teens and into their twenties, and so on.

The inevitable chorus of cynics raised their collective hands about an important issue: data. With the information that Facebook collects from its users – from demographics about how old a person is, where she's from and what school she goes to, plus her likes and dislikes across the site and across the web – the company could also identify people who'd be very valuable to advertisers. You see, that is how Facebook makes its money: it sells your data to people who place ads that are specifically targeted at you. Before June 2011, it didn't have any accurate data about anyone using its service who was under the age of 13. After June 2011, it did. And this data could be sold and used to create an extraordinarily targeted arsenal of advertising that would fuel the pester power artillery.

Here are two of the sides of a many-headed beast that upsets people when you mention "children" and "the web" in one sentence. On the one hand, people think it's important that kids can use the system and have access to this incredibly rich resource. In the UK, "ICT", or Information and Communication Technology, is part of the national education curriculum. Courses teach schoolkids how to use it, and how to be safe and responsible while they're there.

On the other hand, the perception is that the more they go online, the more they're vulnerable to strangers who have bad intentions, and to companies who want to exploit them. This is the bit of the discussion that usually fuels the headlines. In general, no one, except a few researchers, actually knows what kids do online. So those headlines are generally uninformed.

According to the EU Kids Online report, 9–16-year-olds spend almost an hour and a half of their leisure time per day on the web, almost half of that in their bedrooms, and a third via their mobile phones. The only thing it's replacing is television time. The imagined past – the one where families sit around the dinner table discussing their days – was already an eroded reality before the web. So what are they doing? They're mostly on social networking sites, says EU Kids Online, connecting with friends and continuing the play that happens between (and during) classes, which means that the online world has become as valuable a place to learn about who they are and to develop their social skills as school, the playing field or the playroom. The research bears this out: kids use the web as a place to experiment with different identities. They take on different roles in different contexts to see whether they work and whether they fit: sometimes they're in charge; other times, they follow the leader. In online games like Club Penguin, Cyworld or Moshi Monsters, they balance budgets, learn to negotiate with other players (and, yes, manipulate them) and define themselves by their avatars and their virtual rooms. The web for them is a sophisticated sandbox of make-believe where they get to create stories and then join in with friends to act them out. It's not a surprise that many researchers describe these environments as virtual dolls' houses.

What has changed is who might be in the playgroup. Kids today have access to an almost completely open communication platform that allows them to connect with people all over the world, many of whom are going through the same biological, psychological and social changes. Instead of developing a self-identity limited by what they discover in their immediate surroundings in the playground or at the shops, they can now do it on social networks, in networked computer games and via SMS (text messaging).

A point of clarification: when we talk about "kids" online, we're covering a large area. A three-year-old mousing around the CBeebies website has as much in common with a 16-year-old on Facebook as my cat has to my dog: they are, practically speaking, different species. A whole lot of biological, neurological and psychological development goes on in the intervening years, so it's not very useful to talk about "the kids online" as a single entity. While child psychology is fascinating, it's incredibly complex and not my area of expertise. I don't have the capacity to comment on child development and what's going on with their brains: to me, what's more interesting is the effect the web is having on kids' social development. How is the web affecting what they think and do? You can see this most clearly in the group that's going through the biggest social change: adolescents.

Pre-to-late teenage kids get their culture, gossip and attitudes from Google and Facebook. They, more than anyone else, are constantly on, constantly showing off and constantly connected. But are the headlines true? Do they really think filming their mates slapping strangers and then putting the videos up on YouTube is hilarious? Are they really sexting like hormone-fuelled ... well, teenagers? Is everyone a cyberbully, or being cyberbullied? Is this generation of digitally enabled, computer-savvy youth a menace to society, hacking into the mainframes of hallowed institutions? Sure. Some are, some do. And all of them are using the web in the same way my friends and I used the shopping mall: as a third place in which to get together and shape who we are.

Take a step back and try to recall your own generational trans-
gressions. Youth culture, on the surface dominated by musical tastes,
slang, fashion and objectionable hairstyles, is nothing but part of
growing up. It's about expressing yourself, becoming part of a tribe,
making your mark. It's about defining yourself as separate from your
parents and everything that's ever come before, ever. It's also about
finding out where the boundaries of social acceptability lie. It's usually
about reinventing the wheel.

This kind of "youth" first emerged in the 19th century when, as
author Jon Savage described in *Teenage: The Creation of Youth 1875–
1945*, the notion of youth "as a separate, stormy, rebellious stage of
life" began. Although the word "teenager" may have been invented at
the time of James Dean, causing a social meltdown and libraries of
newspaper articles about unwieldy kids and the demise of society, the
phenomenon had already been around for a century. I suppose that's a
little bit like today, when teenage rebellion has taken to the digital age.

Because we grownups can't see what they're doing, we feel
we've lost control. And we can't see the relationship between what's
happening online and how that translates into piercings, hair colour
and incomprehensible slang, so we don't understand what these odd
signals (to our eyes) mean. We're naturally fearful, and when we can see
what they're doing, on Facebook for example, we're horrified, but we
still can't understand what's happening as we are unable to pick up the
subtle, unspoken checks and balances that happen within a subculture
and define the behaviour within it. Remember that adolescence is a
time that is fraught with insecurities and hormone-fuelled emotions.
Professor Livingstone translates: "What young people are doing on
Facebook when they gossip and socialise is intensively monitoring
what everyone else is doing and what everyone else is saying," she

says. She believes that young people are now living in a much more anxious, self-judging way than in previous generations. They're in an always-on world, where there's no downtime without the spectre of their friends watching or listening. "It would be interesting to talk with young people about silences," Livingstone says. "About the pursuit of personal hobbies."

Is there any way to make sense of what teenagers are doing? "Historically there has been a trigger – a music change or style change – that's prompted a variety of different youth adaptations," says danah boyd [sic], co-author of the MacArthur-funded research project *Hanging Out, Messing Around, and Geeking Out*. But now, with so many technological touchpoints and interest-driven groups, there's no single social change that will inspire "youth" to act, at least not as one entity. It was easier to pinpoint an influence when kids mimicked and rallied around television, music and the movies: their attention was clearly focused on one thing, and it influenced how they dressed, spoke and acted. But now attention is an even more difficult thing to quantify and capture, because the way kids consume media is so fragmented. It's easier to cluster age groups by how teenagers are using the web rather than what they're consuming on it. If they're gossiping and socialising, the user is probably a teenager. If it's being used for dating, the person on the other side of the screen is probably in his twenties. And, boyd says, people in other life stages use it in other ways.

What is most surprising about the findings of the research in this field is that, despite the possibilities for connecting with people across the global network, there is actually very little evidence for a common global youth culture. In fact, kids seem to keep their online activity close to home. "Most young people interact with people they know in their everyday environments," says boyd. Yup, even with the possibilities. This does have implications for kids' development. "When you go onto Facebook with teenagers, they live in a world where they think everybody thinks like them," boyd says. Livingstone concurs: "We ever more surround ourselves by people like us who share the same beliefs and values, thoughts and anxieties. There's much less time spent muddling along with people who are really quite different." So rather than a globally homogenised youth culture, there are lots of little tight-knit, homogenous fragments. This is something that is dogging not just kids but the rest of us too, but the tools the kids use – whether they're social networks, blogs, games or YouTube – create more intensive feedback loops than have been experienced before. The social effects of this are as yet unknown, because we've not seen the first generation to grow up with the web graduate into adulthood. "Something transformative is happening," believes Livingstone of the new media. "I don't think it's happened yet."

"Families are not necessarily as physically close as they once were," says Katie O'Donovan, Mumsnet spokesperson, the most popular UK online community for parents. "Certainly a hundred years ago few families would have left their villages or towns, now it's not uncommon for mums and dads to be raising their kids miles from their own mums and dads or aunts and uncles." In fact, throughout the 20th century, more people raised kids on their own than ever before. More women worked away from home. Fertility rates were down, divorce was on the rise. And this, according to something called the *Family Decline Thesis* (what it says on the tin), is leading to community breakdown. What this thesis says is that a family unit of mum, dad and 2.2 kids builds the scaffolding that defines who we become and how we behave. Without it, we struggle to develop basic trust and social capital.

So how much is technology contributing to this trend? Well, there's a school of thought that says technology is actually stepping in and helping families re-engage with one another in a meaningful way. It's bridging the face-to-face gap, making it possible to live apart but still stay close.

We live in an increasingly transient world, where the opportunity to make a living has given rise to mass migration to urban centres in every country around the globe. Children are separated from parents, siblings from one another, and the web makes it easy to stay in touch. In 2008, the Pew Research Center released a report describing how technology is transforming the family unit: "Technology is enabling new forms of family connectedness that revolve around remote cell phone interactions and communal internet experiences," it said. John, a reader of my Untangling the Web newspaper column, wrote in to share his experience.

He has a job that separates him from his kids, aged five to nine, and uses online games and Skype to play with them, read to them and hang out with them for at least an hour a day before bed. "I read about someone's dad, many years ago, playing chess with his son using a velcro board and the postal service," says John, who joined the kids' online game site Club Penguin to do a similar thing with his own children when he's away. "It's about inventiveness. My partner and I share a Club Penguin account; we do up our igloo as a place that is ours for the kids to visit whenever they like."

"The fundamentals of most families have stayed the same," says Mumsnet's O'Donovan. "What's changed are the tools to help us get the most out of our family life." Online activity can deliver an intimacy that families separated by distance might otherwise lose. We are communicating with one another more, and in richer media than before, across the globe. Of course, web-based closeness doesn't replace face-to-face contact. As John's nine-year-old son Josh points out, you can't "have a hug" online, but the time John and Josh share together via the computer is better than nothing, isn't it?

The best news of all, particularly for concerned parents who see their children logging into Facebook and navigating the web, is that the risks that the headlines shout about – the stranger danger, the grooming, the potential harm – have reassuringly low incidence rates. Livingstone and her team identified kids' most frequent risky behaviour, from looking for new friends to connecting with and sending videos or photos of themselves to people they've never met in person, and found that fewer than 15% of kids share videos or photos of themselves, or share personal information like where they live or what their phone numbers are. They also found that 40% use the web to look for new friends and, if something dodgy happens, they'll tell a friend, followed by a parent, and then activate defensive strategies that they've learned in school, from parents or their peers. Kids are responsible online. We have less to fear than we think. "Allow children to experiment online with relationships and identity," says the report. "This is vital for growing up if children are to learn to cope with the adult world." With attention on Facebook and the way it has already entangled 9–12-year-olds, perhaps it's a better idea to let them sign up than to shroud a child's first online experience in secrecy and deceit.

700 FRIENDS ON FACEBOOK

"The paradox we observe is that the Internet is a social technology used for communication with individuals and groups, but it is associated with declines in social involvement and the psychological well-being that goes with social involvement."

INTERNET PARADOX: A SOCIAL TECHNOLOGY THAT REDUCES SOCIAL INVOLVEMENT AND PSYCHOLOGICAL WELL-BEING?

In 1998, Robert Kraut of Carnegie Mellon University and his colleagues published their research on a group of people they had introduced to the web. From 1994 to 1996, they'd asked this group to rate their levels of wellbeing, their feelings of social isolation and the number of friends they had. In this period, while going online, the new web users reported that they had fewer social bonds, felt more depressed and struggled to establish trust in other people in virtuality. How could they be friends with someone? They couldn't even be sure who the other person was.

Newspapers were splashed with the article's subheading, *A Social Technology That Reduces Social Involvement and Psychological Well-Being?* Fanning the flames of fear with this new and untested technology, this research paper is still one of the most frequently cited papers when journalists write about the quality of life online. But according to what we know now, after fifteen years of research that has consistently and almost universally contradicted the findings of the *Internet Paradox*, the web is one of the best places to make new friends and have a rich and rewarding social life in the modern world. When Professor Kraut and his colleagues introduced his 169 brand new web users to this weird new virtual place, there were only 36 million people online worldwide. That's fewer than the number of people who had Facebook accounts in the UK in 2012. Professor Kraut moved his new online residents into the web equivalent of a ghost town.

If you move to a new town where none of your family or friends are, and there's no way to find out where everyone is, of course you're going to feel lonely. It takes a while to settle in, find your butcher, the local park and the doctor's office, and to meet people you feel you can connect with. But you will make friends. After a while, you'll get to know the people you see every day at the corner shop or at the school gates. You'll start to hang out with the people who like the same things as you, who think about the same things and who want to do the same things. You might even make plans to see one another for coffee. You'll gradually start to share things with them, and they'll reciprocate. You'll meet up more often, reveal more about yourself and discover more things you have in common. In time, almost without trying, you'll discover you can't remember when you weren't surrounded by friends – people who provide emotional support and social scaffolding. You'll end up trusting them with all kinds of things: your spare keys, a small cash loan, personal information. You might even think it'd be OK to leave your kids with them. This takes time.

When the data was being collected for the *Internet Paradox* study, between 1995 and 1997, the web wasn't yet a mainstream preoccupation. People had perhaps used it to send "e-mail" but they couldn't navigate it easily, and they very rarely shopped online. Online communities were hard to find and generally they were viewed with scepticism: most stories about virtual friendships in the press were finger-pointing

"No way!" pieces about freaks and geeks who, according to the spin, struggle with social ability already and had escaped to the only place where they could find other inept people like themselves. Four years later, Professor Kraut and his team published an astonishing volte face, *Internet Paradox Revisited*. It's not surprising to see why. By 2002, there were nearly 600 million people online, Google was the main way we made sense of the vast ocean of online information, the dotcom bubble had inflated, sowing a rich e-commerce ecosystem and plenty of online shopping opportunities, and most importantly there were more people in the virtual village to bump into, there was much more to do, and a much richer environment to do it in. Lo and behold, in Professor Kraut's later study, people reported an increase in the number of meaningful, trust-based relationships. By 2002, the online world was helping people make more friends. It also helped them feel less lonely and less depressed. This wasn't a one-off. Almost every research study since that time has pointed in the same direction: online friendships are not only possible, but people feel less socially isolated when they go online. And when the online world and the offline worlds co-exist – for instance, when you hang out on Facebook with people you're connected to at work or school, or you meet up at the pub with people you first encountered online – this effect is even more powerful. The web reinforces friendships with people we already know and people whom we've just met. By 2007 the Oxford Internet Institute reported that almost a quarter of internet users had met someone online whom they readily described as a "friend". And the more we use the web, the truer this becomes.

There are a few rules for making friends. To start with, people have to be in the same space at the same time often enough to register each other's presence. It's a pragmatic thing, but obviously it's essential. Offline, you might bump into someone at a corner shop or a community centre, the workplace or the same part of the park where you walk your dogs. If you turn up every day at 3pm, and so does the other person, you might recognise one another, and maybe eventually get chatting. Online, you're obviously not meeting in a physical location. Instead, it might be a chat room, forum, email list or Twitterfall. Wherever you are, if you go there often enough, people will come to recognise you by your profile name, your picture or your avatar, and this is the first signal that says whether or not you'd get along.

Offline, what you wear tells people a lot about you: perhaps you both happen to be part of the goth subculture and wear black eyeliner, boots, studded necklaces and dye your hair a shocking shade of pink. Online, if you both belong to the Sisters of Mercy fan community, you've already expressed a similar interest. What you choose for a profile picture, or the type of font you choose for your blog, or the theme you choose for your website all give other people little clues about who you are, and whether you might get along. The creative things people call themselves online are also saturated with meaning. Social networks are great at signalling similarity based on common friends: the idea here is that if you and another person know the same people, you're probably like one another in many ways. And then of course there are the things you say that very clearly express your opinions and interests. After a while, someone makes the first move. The dog walkers in the park might start with a comment about the weather or their pet and then eventually ease into something a bit more significant. Work colleagues might exchange pleasantries by the water cooler or at the coffee machine.

There's a virtual version of this getting-to-know-you chit-chat. It's called a status update. "What are you doing now?" asks microblogging service Twitter. Whatever the critics say about the pointlessness of tweeting what you are having for breakfast or that you're stuck in a lift, the research tells us that status updates are an essential ingredient in friendship formation. "Twitter," wrote Oxford researcher Danica Radovanovic in 2012, "is very similar to saying 'what's up?' in an analogue space as you pass someone on the street when you have no intention of finding out what is actually going on."

"Tweets and mundane Facebook updates about weather, food, what you're doing, where are you doing it, and how are actually healthy for the online communities, human relationships, and for sustaining social network systems," she says. Anthropologists in the 1930s called the offline version of this small talk "phatic" communication: "the quality of the information being communicated has no practical value and is rather mundane," Radovanovic says, but it is still heavy with meaning. It tells people you're looking for some kind of social interaction. By making those apparently nonsensical mini-quips, you're sending a signal to the world that you want to make a connection and hoping someone will pick it up.

Oddly, this very public display of what you're doing is one of the ways we develop online intimacy. Reading what your Auntie Ron says about her grandkids and her trip to the supermarket on Facebook means you probably know as much about her day-to-day emotional and physical life as you do about your best mate, whom you only chat with on the phone or see over coffee once a month. You may not see Auntie Ron except at family reunions, but you still have a sense that you are participating in her life. This disconnected connectivity and, in the absence of frequent face-to-face meet-ups, phatic communication seal relationships by reinforcing connections between people. It gives you more to go on as you decide whether or not you trust the other person, and then, if you choose to, you can move on to something more.

People often say that they make friends more quickly online, and that these friends become more significant to them more quickly. According to Professor Aaron Ben-Ze'ev from the University of Haifa, a psychologist who's studied online relationships since 2003, the reason this happens is because people tend to be more open and honest on the web. We feel we can be more ourselves when we're masked by a keyboard and mouse, like when people go to a masquerade ball: we won't hold anything back, and because we're being true, we think other people are too.

On the one hand, we don't think we can trust another person online enough to call him or her a friend, but on the other we're telling them more than we'd tell our closest friends or family. If you've ever sat next to a stranger on a train who's told you every little detail about her life, it's the same kind of thing. We do this because it's the only way to establish a connection with a person who seems unreal, because we can't touch or see or hear or smell them. Each piece of personal information we give to a virtual stranger is like proffering a little olive branch in the hopes that it will lead to a connection across faceless, placeless cyberspace. It's what we do as social creatures. It just happens a bit faster online.

The nuances of the close, emotional bonds that people have with one another have always been difficult to pin down. Those who have studied friendship, like evolutionary anthropologist Robin Dunbar from the University of Oxford, sociologist Claude Fisher at the University of California at Berkeley and the late sociologist Everett Rogers from the

University of New Mexico, have always struggled to identify what it is that makes the distinction between "friend", "pal", "buddy", "chum", "acquaintance", and all of the numerous semantic variations in between. Rogers defines a relationship as more close if people communicate more often. Fisher defines a friendship as close if you feel you can ask the other person for a cash loan. And Dunbar thinks it's about how much time you spend with that person. These are very different definitions of friendship, and all derived from what it is that people have told them is close friendship. A "friend" on Facebook can mean a family member, a best mate, someone you work with, a person you met in the back of a cab on the way from the train station to a hotel, or someone you've never met before but who asked to be your friend because she likes how you spell your name. When people look at Facebook or other social networks and say they're ruining the meaning of friendship, or diluting it in an obstructive and dangerous way, they're not seeing how people distinguish emotional closeness or distance. Online, it's possible to define a connection as more or less close by looking at how often two people communicate, whether they communicate in a public place or behind the scenes (like in a private chat room or via a direct message), how many crossover networks they have and other such behavioural "tells". It's surprisingly easy to see, when you know what to look for, that online friends do vary in emotional closeness. So, although a person may appear to have 700 friends on Facebook, what they really have is both intimate friends and acquaintances.

The technology makes it easier to keep track of more and more people. It helps us stay close, and it brings us closer to strangers more quickly. Does this mean that technology is expanding our social circles in an unprecedented way? Professor Dunbar came up with the "Social Brain

Hypothesis" in 1998. It gives a physiological, evolutionary view of how many friends it is biologically possible to have and, according to this theory, human beings can only maintain 150 meaningful relationships, not 700 friends. Dunbar says this number is limited by the size of our brains: we only have enough brainpower and time in the day to maintain relationships with a small group of people. Our inner circle is made up of fewer than 20 or so of our nearest and dearest and, of that, our closest friends and kin number only around five. Around this core are around 30 acquaintances, and then the final layer – what Dunbar calls the "active network layer" – is filled with the remaining hundred or so "familiars" with whom we're loosely connected.

By 2009, this theory had really only been tested in offline groups. So, curious, *The Economist* asked Cameron Marlow, Facebook's in-house sociologist, to test Dunbar's theory, to see if people can have 700 friends now that technology is such a part of our lives. Marlow grouped people into two chunks: people who had an average of 120 friends and people who had an average of 500 friends. He then looked at how many of their friends they talked to in public (commenting on photos, status updates or on their walls) and in private (messages or chats). Using this as a way to identify closeness between friends (close: public chat; closer: private chat), he found that we really only stay in contact with a few, core people. Regardless of the size of your network, people talk with between ten and 26 Facebook friends in public and between four and 16 Facebook friends in private. Proportionately, this is a very small number out of 120 or 500 people. So, according to this study, Dunbar's Social Brain Hypothesis works online too: there is still a limit of around 10% of the people we know whom we would call part of our inner social circle. The rest we just keep around because they don't take up any cognitive load.

But is Dunbar's hypothesis actually capturing the whole story online? The number of close friends and people in the inner circle has remained proportionately the same, but the number of people we are able to stay in contact with has increased. The people who are just names on a friends list are still there, even if the list numbers more than 150. In the past, we'd have forgotten about them. Now, they exist as people on the edge of human relationships, and this is an edge we're reminded of any time someone out there updates his or her status.

Professor Dunbar's active network layer is in constant flux. Connections are made, which brings people into the layer, and broken, which kicks them out. These are the people we don't see every day, but who we know exist. We remember their birthdays because we get a reminder. and we call on them when we need specialist help, because we remember that they're experts in something and they're easy to reconnect with by poking them or sending them an email. We probably wouldn't ask for a loan or for a shoulder to cry on, but these people are in the backs of our minds. Friends of friends, maybe, or old work colleagues.

Could the web make the social circles we can cope with larger than 150 people? Facebook's great at connecting old school friends, for example. That's actually where most of us say we know our Facebook connections from. These are the ties that, pre-social networks, would be well past their sell-by dates, and the only time they might be rekindled is once every few years at reunions. Now they're in our virtual faces, scribbling on our virtual walls. We are told what their kids look like and where they spent last Friday night. We are reminded of them, so although they wouldn't be included in the active network layer according to Professor Dunbar's theory, those connectives are still active in the era of the virtual revolution.

What function do they serve? Do they bump our friends who don't use digital technologies to keep in touch out of the 150? Oxford researcher Dave White and I describe this as an "exploitation" layer: these folks have social value, although the connections aren't very active. They're like even more distant versions of the people in the active network layer: not close friends at all, but part of our technologically facilitated social consciousness. If we need something that they can provide, we think of them because they're in our peripheral vision. They're like an active network layer feeding pool: they are distant acquaintances whose relationship statuses, favourite movies and latest activities we know, and that's much more than we would have known before.

With the possibility for a technologically enhanced social circle comes a potential downside. I call it "emotional anaemia", the sense that what you're getting from your online social group is emotion-lite. In other words, you might not feel the online love from the people you should, because your nearest and dearest may be drowned out in the ocean of sociability.

It's not because the web can't support strong emotional bonds – we know it can, but the social network world has been designed to help you accrue more and more and more friends. What may eventually happen is that the exploitation and active network layers make too much noise for you to adequately hear your close friends online. Ironically, there were too few people online when the *Internet Paradox* was first published. Now there may be too many, and the result of these polar opposite situations may be the same.

The web is the best friend-forging technology that's ever existed. It's a tool that gives us a richer understanding of who our close relations and family are because of what they put online. It can extend our social lives to include far more people than we've ever thought possible. It's certainly no longer a social technology that reduces social involvement and psychological wellbeing.

But where the *Internet Paradox* does still exist is in how much we value the people who we only know online. The web is an incubator for closeness, but for friendship to be something that can't be switched off on a whim, the relationship also needs some face-to-face time, or at least crossover to other networks and online interactions. Without this, the din of acquaintances and familiars may overwhelm the whisper of something getting closer.

There's a new danger that Robert Kraut and his colleagues didn't consider when they were writing in 1998, in the relative ghost town of the world wide web. Now, because there are so many people online, we are in danger of filtering out potential friends and lovers because they're not friends of friends or people who match the criteria we've selected in a profile.

iLOVE

The web can be great at helping people reinforce relationships, but rather than making the connections between close friends and the folks in the inner core stronger, it seems to be best at bringing acquaintances and familiars closer together. It bumps people up against others who are interested in similar things, and it's also an excellent friend-of-a-friend introducer, so meeting someone you're likely to get on with is much easier now than in the days when we couldn't see the people our friends were friends with, and we weren't wearing our interests like badges on our chests.

We are more likely to want to meet new people at different times in our lives. Young people are outreach machines: they have far more friends than people over the age of 50, and according to a research report by the Oxford Internet Institute from 2011, the virtual friendships kids make will go offline too. Different life circumstances, for example when we move to a new town, start a new job, have kids or end a relationship, also compel us to reach out and touch someone new, and the web is there to make it happen.

But what if we're longing for something a little more than friendship? What's the web doing for the pursuit of love? According to the Oxford Internet Institute survey *Me, My Spouse and the Internet*, the actual "falling in love" bit of the process hasn't changed enormously since we started hanging out online: we still follow the same steps in the "getting to know you" process as we have done for millennia, and we're still looking for trust, honesty and commitment. No, the greatest change is how we find love. "Marriage markets" not only include the web as an avenue to look for potential partners nowadays, but it's becoming the first port of call for many. In the US, the Pew Internet & American Life Project reported in 2008 that 30% of people who use the web and are currently in a relationship say they met through online dating, and 74% of single Americans searching for lovers have used the web to look for a significant other. Social networking sites are now hugely important tools in the love box because they provide a context for a potential match (like being a friend of a friend) and expose unexpected similarities between people based on their shared connections, or the types of things people like. That's a starting point. Once things progress and the relationship is ready to move offline, we're using our online friends, networks and Google to authenticate whether or not we should step out with someone.

Sam Yagan is the charismatic and dynamic CEO and co-founder of OKCupid, the dating site with the largest registered user-base of 18–34-year-olds in the US. "Online dating used to be something that people turned to when they were giving up on offline dating," he says. "It is now a tool that people are turning to, to complement their offline dating." For younger people, it's like running water: of course you add online dating to your list of finding a match. But older people have also taken to it like fish to water, and the *Me, My Spouse and the Internet* OII report says over 50s are disproportionately more likely to try it than use more traditional methods: the fastest-growing group of online daters over the age of 24 is older people looking for love after the breakdown of a long-term relationship or death of a spouse. Why? Because it's easier (and possibly more palatable) to create an online profile than go to a singles bar.

Online dating isn't just for the chronically shy or people who simply can't "do" relationships. "You may be a 23-year-old attractive woman who's getting lots of dates offline, but why not make yourself available to many other people who you might not meet in your day-to-day life?" asks Yagan, whose first passion was mathematics. "Offline dating is constrained by the physical realities of space. You typically date people who are near you, or who are in the same routines that you are. They tend to be very similar to you. Online dating brings you together with people who are different from you, and so you'll get more diverse relationships: in age, neighbourhood, socio economically, everything across the board."

In fact, people who meet online tend to have a greater age difference and come from a wider range of educational backgrounds than people who meet offline, the OII report says. You use your brain to identify a potential mate rather than your emotions. And while offline you'd be more likely to filter someone out because they don't fit your imagined ideal of a Prince or Princess Charming, what someone looks like becomes less important when you find someone who shares your interests. Capulets and Montagues be damned! Like the star-crossed Romeo and Juliet, it doesn't matter where you come from, it's all about finding the right person for you.

A lot of the graft and uncertainty has been removed from the process: online dating systems are built to deliver, and they do this by throwing a tsunami of possibilities at your virtual front door and seeing what sticks. People looking for love are literally drowning in opportunities. By Yagan's calculations, this leads to a better success rate: "If you spend a couple of months looking through a pool of two million people, you can feel pretty confident that when you choose someone, they're a perfect match for you," he says. Think what you will about love and romance; we're still looking for the same things, but we've become a bit more businesslike about it.

There's no better example of this than the plethora of services that help people scratch very specific itches. As Nick Paumgarten reported in *The New Yorker* in 2011, some online dating sites "add an extra layer of projection and interpretation; they adhere to a certain theory of compatibility, rooted in psychology or brain chemistry or genetic coding, or they define themselves by other, more readily obvious indicators of similitude, such as race, religion, sexual predilection, sense of humor, or musical taste." There are dating sites for people who like their lovers in uniform (uniformdating.com), who want a Sugar Daddy (Sugardaddie.com), who have kids (DatingforParents.com), who have degrees (loveandfriends.com), who are Jewish (JDate.com) or Christian (ChristianMingle.com), who are Indian (shaadi.com) and many, many more. The total revenue for the US alone in 2008 was $957 million, according to analytics company Forrester Research. It isn't going to go away; this industry is bigger than online porn.

It may seem ironic that a cold, logical computer has become an important mediator for the warmest and fuzziest of human emotions, but mediated love isn't a new thing. Elizabeth Barrett Browning fell in love with her future husband Robert via letter between 1845 and 1846, and the telegraph ushered in its fair share of love affairs around the time that our modern concept of romance first emerged. Tom Standage describes the first "online" wedding between a bride in Boston and a groom in New York in 1848 in *The Victorian Internet*: "At the appointed hour [the bride] was at the other end of the wire in the Boston telegraph office and, with the telegraph operators relaying their words to and fro in Morse code, the two were duly wed by the magistrate." Terribly romantic, no?

Almost 150 years later, the first web-based marriage took place between Andy (from Somerset, England) and Lisa (from Palm Beach,

Florida). The pair had been introduced by a mutual virtual friend in a chat room on Saturday 25th May 2006. "It was after only a week of chatting online that I asked Lisa to come over to visit me in England," says Andy. It worked. Lisa moved to the UK in July, and the pair were engaged within a week. Four months later, they were married: the bride and groom were in a cybercafe in Taunton in Somerset in England, and the officiant, the Reverend Mike Bugal, was sitting at his computer in Seattle, Washington in the USA. Another Reverend was due to bless the marriage from his computer in Lyndhurst, England at 8pm, but a broken cable wiped out all of Taunton's telecommunications at exactly that time, delaying events: "More frantic phone calls with BT eventually managed to secure a standard telephone link with the Internet," explains the couple's homepage. "After over two hours of waiting, the blessing could finally re-commence." The congregation, logged into the #cyberwedding chat room from all corners of the globe, watched and read as <RevMike> typed, "Will you take Andrew (^Cloud9) to be your wedded husband? Will you love, comfort, honour and respect him?" and Lisa responded, "I will."

Despite the technological hiccups that caused <RevMike>'s internet connection to repeatedly log him out of IRC chat in the middle of the proceedings, the two promised to "share all life has to offer both online and IRL (in real life) together", and were congratulated by the hundreds of people who attended the celebration, and whom they knew from the web but had never met in the flesh before.

Andy's and Lisa's whirlwind love affair is pretty typical of an online romance. Because we invest so much emotion, expectation and idealisation in the objects of our virtual affections, web-based love affairs tend to feel hyper-intense, hyper-quickly. And because there are so many blanks we have to fill in, we can over-enhance a partner's positive features and make up the rest to meet our romantic ideals. The fantasy, of course, can be different from the reality. OK Cupid's 1.5 million active users are actually on average two inches shorter than they say on their profiles. They generally earn 20% less than they report, and "the more attractive the picture, the more likely it is to be out-of-date," says OKCupid's OKTrends blog. Only 20% of reported bisexuals actually are bisexual. Of course, these little white lies happen offline too: "Regardless of medium, there's always going to be an element of marketing whenever you're going to meet someone new," says Yagan. But if you want to get some attention in this new marketplace, it helps to know the rules.

The most important rule: "it's the best writers who get laid," says Julian Dibbell in *My Tiny Life*, which he wrote about the popular online community from the 1990s, LambdaMOO. "Well-rounded, colourful sentences start to do the work of big brown soulful eyes," he says. "Too many typos in a character's description can have about the same effect as dandruff flakes on a black sweater." Clearly, if you're on the prowl online, it pays to get a skilled ghostwriter.

The second rule: balance personal marketing and reality. As a friend with the most popular profile on the *Guardian*'s Soulmates dating service for several months discovered, you can be too awesome: always include a few warts. His profile was crafted by two friends who took it upon themselves (without Nick's knowledge) to add him to the online dating pool. Both happen to be professional writers, which is, perhaps, why he was at the top of the pile for many for so long. And although Nick is an impressive guy, he felt he didn't live up to the version of himself that his friends had created. He never felt quite as funny and quick with words as his dates expected. "People cannot lie about constitutive personal features, such as a sense of humour, wittiness, and personal interests, all of which emerge during lengthy online conversations," says Professor Ben-Ze'ev.

We are looking for certain things in a relationship partner, and these are surprisingly close to things we've looked for since the first computer-mediated dating service was invented in 1965. In heterosexual couples, women on the whole want a man who is of a higher socioeconomic status with a good track record, while men are looking for extremely good-looking women who have low-paying jobs. If we need any evidence for this, Professor Monica Whitty at the University of Leicester has been studying an online relationship scam that is thought to have hit up to 230,000 people since it came to the attention of serious crime organisations in 2008. She says the profiles that are used to reel in victims fall into exactly this pattern. But what's a good track record? What's "extremely" good-looking? The dating algorithms can bump us up against people who fit these very loose and non-specific criteria, and can filter out prospects based on our other preferences, but there's still a value judgment that we have to make ourselves before we decide if a match is successful or not. And sometimes we might be delightfully surprised by the totally unexpected.

Now, I'm not a fan of the idea of being matched with someone based on some kind of algorithmically determined compatibility. I don't have a lot of faith in psychological tests in general, and so don't really want something that's one step removed to help me find a potential match. As Nick Paumgarten said in *The New Yorker*, "There are [online dating sites] which basically allow you to browse through profiles as you would boxes of cereal on a shelf in the store. Others choose for you; they bring five boxes of cereal to your door, ask you to select one, and then return to the warehouse with the four others. Or else they leave you with all five."

The online tick-boxes scene isn't for me. Rather, I'm a fan of serendipity and those accidental, delightful encounters that change the course of your life. I don't even like to search for friends on Google because I prefer first-hand impressions rather than machine-determined information. Perhaps I am romantically attached to the idea of the "reveal": looking at someone else's digital bits means that you might overlook something wonderful because of something that might not be a deal-breaker later in the relationship but it seems important at the outset. Online dating sites are looking for ways to hook you up, but they're using pattern-matching techniques that are anything but serendipitous. We're limiting our opportunities by finding out too much beforehand, and the web is making the happy accident obsolete.

In a 2009 report for the world's biggest online dating conglomerate, Match.com, Professor Whitty and her research team found that more than half of women and 43% of men have become fussier about who they date. This is a trend, they say, that's increasing year on year. And the OII's research has found that people have become more "instrumentally focused [...] increasingly considering the practice of finding a mate as a distinct and intentional activity with its own sets of contexts and conventions, rather than something that 'just happens' as one goes about other activities." The dating market has indeed become a market. And it doesn't just cater to single people: infidelity is on the rise. "Online seduction is just a click away," says Professor Ben-Ze'ev.

There are plenty of online services for frisky folk looking for others right now. Grindr.com offers a hugely popular app for gay men to locate their nearest Mr Right Now when the urge comes a-calling, and the online dating scene features a treasure chest of combinations of people who are either already partnered up or who are themselves interested in being the bit on the side. They also cater to relationship needs that range from quickies to something longer-term.

Even if the hanky-panky stays online, it can have consequences for existing offline relationships. "When people start desiring others online their partner will most likely construe this as an act of infidelity," says Professor Whitty. It's not just the act of cybersex that upsets people. Infidelity can be viewed as any time and desire being taken away from the partner. In the OII research, it is very clear what partners approve and disapprove of: heterosexual men and women and gay men and women don't like it when their other halves discuss personal information and their relationship with someone whom they find attractive. And no one wants their partner to be having cybersex or having an emotional relationship with someone else online, even if they are.

But cyberinfidelity is on the rise because, frankly, it's easy and because it tends to be rationalised as less significant than an offline love affair. Professor Whitty found that even in scenarios in which it was clear that a partner had been betrayed, it can still be passed off as "just a friendship" or "mere flirtation". The person on the other side of the screen is only a virtual object, not a real human being, Whitty's participants say. The relationship was exclusively online, they say, and there was never any intention to take it offline.

And people who do cybercheat think an online affair is preferable to a regular romp with a mistress in a hotel room. According to Professor Whitty, "it's not so easy to indulge in one's fantasies of perfection in an offline affair as one has to still deal with the 'real' person." A virtual lover is so much more attractive because the blanks can be filled in according to what you want to believe, and if something turns up that doesn't match the fantasy, the online affair can be turned off with the click of a button.

*

There's a big difference now in the age of the internet. Our romances aren't curated by human matchmakers, but algorithms, and we're falling in love via machine, not via candlelight. We may have a greater hit-rate, but it's not particularly romantic, is it? We mustn't blame the technology: online dating sites may have been developed to do this because we demanded it. We have always clustered into like-minded groups of people, and we've always looked to friends to matchmake. But by letting the machine do this for us, we may be ignoring the possibilities that the web uniquely offers, not to mention the fact that it also has the potential to divide us, rather than bring us together.

iHATE

In the summer of 1996, I was the perpetrator of online hate. It wasn't particularly serious in any way – I was a kid messing around, being an idiot for my own amusement. Of course, compared with the stream of insults that modern day Xbox Live players encounter on a regular basis, my expressions of online hate were pretty tame – I didn't question anyone's sexuality, make any racial slurs or say anything particularly negative about anyone's mother. But still, I had free rein and I totally enjoyed it. I could do anything, say anything, be anything and no one could stop me. The people I was pissing off, whose leisure time I was making unpleasant, were as faceless as I was. They didn't mean anything to me; I didn't care who they were. They could have been robots or figments of my imagination; I was vapour in the digital ether.

I'd logged into my first chat room on the early world wide web. It was an AOL hangout, a general discussion area. It was my first time and, being in that strange interim period between childhood and adulthood, I was finding out the boundaries of being a decent online citizen. Of course, on the web, there seemed to be none, so I started to interrupt, to pick on people, to find their buttons so I could push them. I was briefly the biggest bully on the East Coast of the US. And you know what? It felt bloody good.

But, seriously. I did nothing that actually hurt anyone, at least not that I can tell. It wasn't a prolonged campaign – I didn't track anyone down in real life, I didn't promote violence or extremist ideas and I didn't cause personal harm or even threaten anyone. I was just an arse.

I fell victim to a very light case of the "Online Disinhibition Effect",
an ailment that afflicts some people when they become anonymous,
particularly in situations when there's no authority. My actions were
ultimately hate-lite, nothing like what you might read in the papers.
A headline you read on the front page screaming, "Internet 'terror
breeding ground'" is actually terrifying. It implies that the web
eradicates morality. But how real is this threat? Or is it just tapping into
a public fear in order to sell copies?

In 2012, the UK Home Affairs Committee released an extensive review
of the effects of the web on extremist attitudes and behaviour. It was
called *Roots of Violent Radicalisation*, and in it, the web – along with
universities and prisons – was identified as one of the three places that
was particularly effective at incubating hate in the modern age. The press
picked up on this and, despite the thoughtful and balanced treatment
the authors gave to this incredibly complex and nuanced issue, the
internet was pinpointed on the front pages of many newspapers as
"particularly dangerous" and "one of the few unregulated spaces where
radicalisation is able to take place". In fact, that's not the whole story.
There has been hate since before Cain took out his brother Abel, and,
unsurprisingly, psychologists have been called in to figure out the hate
problem for a long time.

The uncharacteristic behaviour that happens when people have
a feeling of total, consequence-free anonymity has a name. It's
"deindividuation", which means, literally, to be removed from identity.
It's about feeling like your role is inconsequential, like you're lost in the
crowd. As Philip Zimbardo of Stanford University poetically put it in a
1969 research paper, deindividuation is to be "in a state of organism".
What it means is, like my antics in the chat room or the hooliganism

of some football fans in the stadium, people feel less personally responsible for their actions and do things that are impulsive, irrational and normally restricted by their inhibitions. Professor Zimbardo's initial findings were based on an experiment he did at Stanford in the late 1960s. He recreated an infamous study that looked at why people do things that seem inhuman, but manipulated one specific feature: participants' sense of deindividuation.

The original study was conducted by Stanley Milgram in the mid-1950s and it was trying to understand conformity. Milgram, like many other people, was horrified by the events of the Second World War, and wanted to know why people who appeared to be perfectly normal did profoundly inhuman things. So he set up a very simple experiment: one person, the "teacher", was given a list of general knowledge questions. He was seated in a room with an intercom and a large "shock box" machine that had a series of twenty toggle switches that described the voltage and the danger level for each. The voltage started at 0 (low) and went up to 450 (dangerous). The teacher's job was to test a person in the other room on the answers to the questions via the intercom. For every incorrect answer a student gave, the teacher was to push the button, administering a brief electric shock, and then hit the next toggle to increase the voltage for the next incorrect answer. An assistant wearing a lab coat was in the teacher's room throughout the experiment. As the study continued, those answering the questions appeared to become more and more distressed – breathing heavily, screaming, pleading – until they stopped responding completely, but still the shocking went on.

What those teachers administering the shocks didn't realise was that the people answering the questions were actually part of the study; they were not being shocked. It was someone on the other side of the intercom with a tape recorder, playing the sound of someone answering the questions and increasingly becoming distressed. The real experiment was to see whether a person would obey authority even when the actions conflicted with his or her conscience. Milgram and his team had only expected a few people to go all the way to 450 volts – 10%, at a stretch. In fact, 65% of people administered the maximum voltage, and the results of this classic experiment weren't a one-off: the experiment has been replicated countless times, and every time, the results are consistent. Between 61 and 66% of teachers will do what they're told, regardless of time or place, and they'll do it to the bitter end.

So what does this have to do with anonymity and deindividuation? Well, Professor Zimbardo's clever twist was to split the group of teachers in two: one group wore cloaks and hoods, removing any identifying features. The other group wore name tags and their own clothes. The results were consistent with Milgram's study: around 65% of the teachers shocked their students to apparent death. But what was actually being tested was one crucial variable: the people who were "anonymised" – the ones dressed in cloaks and hoods – administered longer and more intense shocks than those who were "individuated" – the ones who wore name tags and their own clothes. By losing their identity, Zimbardo's subjects were more cruel. Some might even call them inhuman.

Zimbardo's experiment was a turning point in this line of research, and there was a decade of psychological experimentation that found similar results: deindividuation led to uninhibited and usually antisocial behaviour. Become part of the organism and you lose your humanity.

Not everyone turns into an idiot online. Of course, it might be because we're not being asked by an authority figure to do something that conflicts with our humanity. But enough people are cruel on the web that there are now dedicated teams in law enforcement and at schools in the UK specifically tasked with combatting cyberhate. Even before the internet, however, some researchers recognised that anonymity didn't lead automatically to cruelty. Occasionally there were even some results showing that deindividuated people performed acts of kindness.

In 1979, psychologists Robert Johnson and Leslie Dowling decided to find out why. They re-ran Zimbardo's experiment with yet another twist: they asked half of their participants to wear outfits that looked like Ku Klux Klan hoods and capes and half to wear nurses' uniforms. Everything else was the same. Teachers still shocked people to apparent death, but the people wearing the Klan outfits were more likely to do so, while those dressed as nurses weren't.

This result tells us that there's actually an interaction between our deindividuated selves and the environment we are in. What we pick up in our surroundings, even if there's very little to go on, and how we interpret those things affects how we will react when we're in a state of "organism". Online expressions of hatred are therefore as much a result of the cultures of Facebook, Twitter, Mumsnet and extremist forums as they are of anonymity. We are not inevitably antisocial when we go online, but some parts of the web have devolved into spaces where it's acceptable to trade insults and to blow off steam. Never read YouTube comments. It's just not worth it.

To try to counteract this kind of behaviour, there's a trend among online community developers, from social networks to news organisations, to try to "re-individuate" users and reduce the online disinhibition effect: they're asking people to register with and be known by their real names. Services like Facebook take this a step further by requiring not only a real name but also an offline network of connections. When you sign up for Facebook you have to submit an official email address associated with an organisation and you have to have at least one network to validate your identity. This way, the theory goes, antisocial behaviour will have real-life consequences. Of course, there are high-profile incidents of cyberbullying on Facebook too, so perhaps re-individuation isn't the answer. In fact, there is no conclusive evidence that tying a person's online identity to their offline self, or their offline social networks, reduces incidents of online hate. Dr John Suler is the theorist who defined the Online Disinhibition Effect, and he believes there are many causes for acts of online hate, not just anonymity. People feel invisible; there's no sense of an overall authority to tell them what to do. They have expectations about what other people will do based on what they *want* them to do. And, ultimately, this whole conversation could all be imagined. They could be communicating with a robot. It could all be in their head. It happens more often than you'd think.

Internet trolls and flame wars can be avoided or ignored. What's really of greater concern is whether the technology encourages mob behaviour, extremism and campaigns of hatred that spill over into offline life. For hatred to fester, online or off, it requires a target. And all communities, online or off, have enemies. They're the people or things that represent the biggest threat to a group but, at the same time, bring it closest together. Having a common enemy means having a mutual understanding of what being part of that community isn't: this could be symbolic or real, like a military threat from an outside territory or an erstwhile friend who's broken the bonds of trust. The point is that a person or thing that a group decides is an enemy represents a kind of collective understanding of what belonging to a group means – what being a group member is and what it isn't.

Many online communities have a moment in their histories when the idealistic, everyone-gets-along fantasy is suddenly burst by an intruder, like I did in the AOL chat room.

Journalist Julian Dibbell had become interested in a popular internet community in the mid-1990s called LambdaMOO. This particular online group created their consensual hallucination using text only, telling stories about who they were and where they were located in cyberspace. Mostly, they just chatted with one another and hung out online. Like many idealistic communities – from the utopias dreamed up by social theorists and put into action by social revolutionaries throughout history – they thought they were immune to outside threats. They thought they'd cracked the answer to social conflict. And then one day it happened.

Dibbell captured the whole rupture in his provocatively titled article for *The Village Voice*. He called the incident, "A Rape in Cyberspace".

One of the members of LambdaMOO called himself "Mr Bungle". He wasn't a particularly popular person in this community, and was more or less known as a troll, or someone who throws out provocations for the sake of it, but that day Mr Bungle crossed a line that hadn't been crossed in this community before. He entered the largest chat area in LambdaMOO and hacked into the accounts of two of the more popular members, Iegba and Starsinger, operated by a woman in Seattle, Washington and a woman in Haverford, Pennsylvania. As everyone in the room, including the two women who operated the accounts, watched, Mr Bungle described the incredibly graphic and indecent sexual acts that he "forced" them to perform on one another and on Mr Bungle himself. The owners of the two accounts were powerless to do anything – they couldn't even log out of the virtual world. They, like the rest of the group, had to sit and watch until Mr Bungle got bored and left the room. And with that, Mr Bungle became Enemy Number One in LambdaMOO.

The next day, the two people whose accounts were hacked and many members of the rest of the community, with the notable absence of Mr Bungle, once again gathered together in the largest virtual communal room to decide what, if anything, they could do. At the forefront of their minds was what kind of punishment they, a group of like-minded, left-leaning, liberal types, should inflict on the perpetrator. Let it slide, or sentence him to the virtual equivalent of the death penalty by banning him from logging in again as Mr Bungle?

After a lengthy debate that lasted several days, they decided to ban him and, in doing so, they defined what kind of behaviour was acceptable as a member of the community and what wasn't. They clarified their boundaries and, as Dibbell wrote, "turned a database into a society."

This apparently innocuous incident on a computer in the early 1990s is replicated online almost every day, even today.

With hindsight, we can see how optimistic the people who populated the early internet were. They believed that the technology would expose how trivial our apparent differences are and lead us to greater global social harmony. After all, how can you hate someone because of their skin colour, nationality, religion, gender or sexuality if you discover a mutual affinity for the same kind of comedy (as expressed through silly cat videos) or the music of Swedish jazz pianist Jan Johansson? Rather than creating a global group hug, we're coping with the vast information and possibilities online by going tribal.

We have a natural propensity to settle into the comforts of what we like to hear and what confirms our existing attitudes. Web technologies and applications like social networks and newsfeeds are happy to serve this desire by filtering out people and information that contradict what we believe, so, online, we're communicating more and more with people like ourselves. This phenomenon is called cyberbalkanisation.

The danger is that, in divorcing ourselves from attitudes we don't like, we become more likely to see the people and the groups who hold those attitudes as different from us. This "us" and "them" attitude is the source of discrimination and hate.

Professors Tom Postmes, Martin Lea and Russell Spears have been studying how we scan our social environments to find people like us, and how we use what we find there to figure out how to behave in a crowd. For more than a decade, they have tested how seemingly irrelevant cues in online interactions become immensely important in who we think another person is. In the deindividuated online space, how quickly someone types, what gender they say they are, which football team they support (which they may have mentioned in passing in a comment months before) will trigger a sense that someone is similar to us, making it more likely that we'll agree with what they say and that we'll do the same things they do. The more we identify who we are by aligning ourselves with the groups we belong to (online or off), the more likely we are to agree with and act upon what we assume are the "appropriate" attitudes and behaviours. While this happens offline too, Postmes, Spears and Lea say that the sparseness of the web makes it more likely that we'll align ourselves to one group based on tiny clues of perceived similarity.

Once we've identified our tribe through the little interpersonal tells, we may fall prey to something called pluralistic ignorance – the belief that everyone else thinks as we do. Generally we're only aware of this phenomenon when it's challenged – when we are surprised to discover that a friend really dislikes something we like, for example, or holds an opinion totally different from our own – but it happens consistently online as well as off.

On the web, however, because we have so many potential contacts located far and wide, and our interactions are generally so focused around specific interests, we tend to assume that everyone else is like us, that everyone agrees with everyone else and, in fact, that everyone else is more dedicated to the cause than we are. We also have less evidence to contradict this. We don't know why pluralistic ignorance is more pronounced online than offline, but there are several studies dedicated to looking at what people think their group thinks, compared with what the group actually thinks, and this really is the case.

In practice, what this means is that if you're part of a group that thinks the *Twilight* series is the best thing ever, you actually think your attitude to the books is pretty tame compared with everyone else's. As Magdalena Wojcieszak found by studying neo-Nazi forums, this effect inspires people to increase their extremism to conform to what they believe everyone else's attitudes to be. The same goes for environmentalists, by the way. In other words, haters – and lovers – fall into step with a misperceived ideal.

It's increasingly easy for online hate groups to play on this. Rather than offer balanced opinions from around the web, they create havens of "safe" content, curated to fit their ideologies. And as online networks with similar attitudes connect across geographical space, they create an inflated sense that their brand of prejudice, discrimination and hate is entirely normal.

That can spur some people on to violent and hateful real-world acts, as the Home Affairs Committee's report concluded, but even the most thorough investigations into the causes of radicalisation point out how little we really know about its origins, online or off. Although the internet can be used to reach an enormous audience unrestricted by geographical boundaries, there's nothing to suggest that it turns people into radicals, unless they are already vulnerable, and vulnerability is a trait that is very difficult to pin down. What we do know is that the internet doesn't make someone vulnerable, but if a person already is, the web can feed that.

Another important finding of the Home Affairs Committee review is that hate groups know the web isn't a great recruitment vehicle. Hate sites are generally inward-looking places where groups define what their boundaries are and what they believe in, rather than places where they try to get new people to sign up. The counter-radicalisation thinktank Quilliam says conversations on Arabic language jihadist forums, for example, are ongoing exercises in clarification, usually involving the outing of members who are felt not to live up to the community's ideal. They're more about making enemies of one another by defining and redefining their boundaries than trying to bring new people, whom they're generally wary of, into the fold. Online radicalisation activities are never successful on their own. Like making friends online, when it comes to fomenting hate, it's important to have some face-to-face time. Radicalisation of vulnerable people that starts on the web is always accompanied by some kind of offline activity.

The web can also be used to dismantle hatred. Dr Karen Douglas from the University of Kent believes that, just as the web is a powerful tool to get the message out, it can also be used to expose flaws behind certain attitudes and destabilise hate groups from the inside.

People who wish to promote hate have a new platform on which to do it, but so do the rest of us. We can use the same platform to debunk their myths. The key is to make sure that the communication technology is used to expose people to a huge variety of information, rather than the fraction of information that the hate group wants to share.

So when Facebook was too slow to remove the group "Israel is not a country! ... Delist it from Facebook as a country!" from their system, the people took over. The group had managed to attract almost 50,000 members between 2007 and 2008. Under the banner of the Jewish Internet Defence League, protestors infiltrated the group, they populated it with pro-Israel messages and evidence that contradicted the anti-Israel propaganda, and eventually drove enough of the original members away to get it shut down.

In 2011 and 2012, an American fast food restaurant discovered that what it did behind the scenes was fair game. Chick-Fil-A's charitable arm actively supported anti-gay charity groups that had been listed as hate groups by the American non-profit civil rights organisation, the Southern Poverty Law Center. Gay rights campaigners took this information and spread it around the web, organising offline protests and gaining the support of politicians. The opposite side hit back, showing its own support by galvanising its proponents online, but eventually the pressure that the fast food chain experienced was enough that it ceased donating to organisations that promoted discrimination against homosexuals and transgendered people.

Not only is it possible but, in some cases, it's absolutely necessary.

Most people believe that they are un-recruitable, un-convinceable and right in all things, and that everyone else is vulnerable, weak-minded and a potential threat. Most people are half right. Despite the seemingly overwhelming power of the internet, we remain human beings.

Looked at rationally, we can understand that it is the context of a communication that gives it its real meaning, and that while we naturally seek the shelter of those like us, actually having our minds radically changed is almost impossibly hard. Our natural wariness, both of people and ideas, is the very thing that prevents radicalisation.

As much as we feel powerless and threatened by what we feel is happening to us online, we have the ability and the resources to fight against the things we feel are wrong. Insight and rationality are the greatest weapons against online hate. And, thankfully, we have a lot of both.

UNTANGLING SOCIETY

Tom Standage is digital editor at *The Economist*. In 1998, he described an extraordinary invention: "A new communications technology was developed that allowed people to communicate almost instantly across great distances, in effect shrinking the world faster and further than ever before. A worldwide communications network whose cables spanned continents and oceans, it revolutionised business practice, gave rise to new forms of crime, and inundated its users with a deluge of information. Romances blossomed over the wires. Secret codes were devised by some users, and cracked by others. The benefits of the network were relentlessly hyped by its advocates, and dismissed by the sceptics. Governments and regulators tried and failed to control the new medium. Attitudes to everything from newsgathering to diplomacy had to be completely rethought. Meanwhile, out of the wires, a technological subculture with its own customs and vocabulary was establishing itself."

He was talking about the telegraph.

I was introduced to Standage's book, *The Victorian Internet*, in 2003 by a colleague in the Digital World Research Centre in the psychology department at the University of Surrey. Lynn described it as a great, accessible read that put the public hysteria about the web into perspective. And it did. It was exactly the long view I needed to begin on my pathway to extract the rhetoric from the reality. Since Lynn first inspired me with her recommendation, I've hoovered up similar books, like Carolyn Marvin's *When Old Technologies Were New*, which looks at the public's reaction to the telephone and the ways people tried to control it.

Standage's and Marvin's books look at things that we are so concerned about with the introduction of new mass market invention: love and romance, personal and national security, and institutions like education, economics, politics and faith, family and community. They remind us that inventions that came before were once "hailed as a means to solving the world's problems", as Standage puts it. The telegraph was going to create a worldwide community and one intellectual neighbourhood; the telephone would annihilate space and time and accelerate global homogenisation. Now, here we are again, pinning our hopes and fears on new technology. Judging by the latest headlines about the web – regardless of whether they think it will save the world or destroy it – it seems that we haven't learned our lessons. We need a reality check when it comes to the 21st century's defining technology.

The problem we're grappling with is that we are too tangled up in the web, experiencing the social and psychological evolutions as they happen. We're so fearful of what it will do to us and our institutions that we forget that we have the power to shape it ourselves.

iHIDE

As I wrote earlier in this book, if you stick "Aleks Krotoski" into an online search engine, you'll be able to learn a lot about me. Along with basic biographical details such as where I was born and who my parents are, you can find out where I've worked, where I've lived, who I hang out with, who I'm close to, that I have a cat (and what his name is), what I like to do at the weekends, what kinds of food I like, and my email address and mobile phone number. Although in social network profiles I tend to hide behind an old close-up of a shock of pink hair (I dyed it until 2009), you'll easily find what I look like from the snapshots that I and others have taken and uploaded, dating mostly from the last ten years but also from college and high school.

With a little more digging, you'll be able to figure out who's in my extended family and what they do, where they live and what they're interested in. You can easily find my home address. You might be able to get a sense of my routine – when I'm in my house and when I'm out. You'll probably know when I'm on work trips. You might be able to pick up on which running routes are my favourites, and on which days and at what times I tend to follow those paths. It would, frankly, be easy to find me, if you were so inclined. Please don't. But you can.

In fact, if someone I didn't know wanted to gain my trust, it'd be pretty easy to find out all this personal information and then spin it into a yarn. They might be online scammers who are trying to exploit me. They might be commercial services that want me to feel an emotional attachment to their brand. And that's just using the information that we put out there ourselves. Imagine what's in a company's database. Imagine what's available to the people who own a website that's built to help you make connections with friends and share personal information between one another, so the site not only has the things you've put into it, but also the things your friends have put into it as well. Surely such a thing would be unthinkable, but of course, it's not.

Facebook should be your worst nightmare. Global privacy watchdog Privacy International have repeatedly voted it the second worst perpetrator of "substantial and comprehensive privacy threats", beaten to the bottom only by search engine Google. Its more than one billion users upload a total of 300 million photos every day to the network, and share intimately personal information about themselves. Of course, Facebook users might manipulate their settings so their information is open only to "friends" – that loose term that covers anyone from a close relative to someone you met last night at the pub – but all of it is available to the company. And it's the stuff behind the scenes that's really extraordinary.

In 2001, an Austrian law student called Max Schrems asked Facebook to give him a copy of all of the personal information on his account. He had a right to request it because he was a foreign national. At that time, people in the US and Canada didn't have this right of access. According to current European law, every country with a headquarters in Europe is obliged to deliver this information upon request. Facebook had to hand this data over, reminded of this by the Irish Data Protection commissioner in September 2011, where the company has its international headquarters.

Schrems had been using Facebook for three years, and already the website had accrued enough information about his activities to fill a 1,200-page dossier. It included details about when he had activated, deactivated and reactivated his account, who he had "friended" and "defriended", who he had "poked" and been "poked" by, the events he had been invited to and how he had replied, the personal email address he had given when activating his account, other personal email addresses that he had not provided himself but that had been associated with his account when his friends uploaded their contacts lists, plus his mobile phone number, all past messages and chats – including the ones he'd deleted – everything he had ever put into the Facebook search box, and account details of other users who had logged onto Facebook on the same computer. In total, there were 57 categories of data in this document alone. Another 80-page document, which he requested separately, added 33 more categories of information on file, including the videos he had posted on his wall, the things he had "liked" on other websites that were linked back to Facebook, and physiological details for facial recognition software to help other Facebook users tag him in photographs they had uploaded. Schrems began an EU-wide campaign to get Facebook to change its service. In Germany, the company was accused of "illegally compiling a vast photo database of users without their consent". The WP29, a group of privacy regulators from across the EU, got involved, the Irish Data Privacy Commissioner audited the website and, in September 2012, Facebook changed its policy to allow anyone – including people in the US and Canada – to access their personal file, and switched off the facial recognition facility in the EU.

At the moment, most of us are only slightly concerned about the implications of the web for our personal privacy. It's an issue for the chattering classes, and most of them continue to have their discussions online. But, like dating, privacy is another of the few areas of our lives that is being transformed by the web. There are several issues at play in the online privacy debate. First is how much we give up about

ourselves to one another and to companies, and what it is about the
technology that increases our willingness to do so. Second is how
much we're tracked by online services, and what responsibility the
companies feel to protect their customers' individual rights. Third is a
growing and fascinating issue: what happens when the databases that
individual companies own are combined with other databases to create
super-databases that can be used to create a profile so powerful that it
can predict what a person will think and do? Finally, what will be the
weakest link in the future: ourselves, corporations, governments or our
friends? Before we descend into doomsday scenarios, let's take a step
back to define what privacy is in the first place.

Privacy is about control. It's not about actual control, according to
web theorist danah boyd [sic]: it's about the perception of control that
individuals think they have over their personal information. Most
people have at least one story to tell about the time when they discovered
how easy it is to give out or to access something that should have been
left hidden. You accidentally hit "send" on an email or instant message,
you made a private tweet public, you discovered a photo of yourself
tagged on a social network, or you did an ego-search on Google and
discovered how much the rest of the world is able to see about you. In
those situations, the information that was put out there ended up in a
different context from the one you expected. Something went wrong
and you lost the control you thought you had over the stuff that you
never really had control of in the first place.

When it comes to personal information, context is king. A person
might be willing to share what they had for breakfast on Twitter, divulge
where they are via FourSquare or report every keystroke made on their
computers since 1998 to their friends. They wouldn't, however, want

information about what happened at the party the night before to land in front of their boss's eyes, or the health visitor to find out about their daily fry-up, or anyone except for trusted friends and family to know where their children are.

The problem isn't the simple act of sharing this information: the problem is who (or what) we choose to share it with, what they do with it and where it turns up. "People seek privacy so that they can make themselves vulnerable in order to gain something: personal support, knowledge, friendship," boyd says. Keeping things back runs counter to a cultural drive: we exchange information in order to develop trust bonds that will allow us to rely on other people for survival, and to advance our societies. What we gain online by divulging our email addresses, credit card details, locations and, yes, what we had for breakfast, is the answer to our question, a way to save time, or a place to keep in touch with old friends and make new ones.

Our views about what should and shouldn't be private vary with cultural and personal conditions. "Things that are very much matters of privacy in one culture won't appear as an issue in another," says digital anthropologist Lane DiNicola. How old are you? Do you live at home? Are you single, married, divorced? Do you have a supportive family? Do you live in an authoritarian or democratic regime? How much social legitimacy you can you claim on the basis of your wealth, race and status?

Social status is actually an important part of the privacy discussion. People higher up the heap have always been able to better manage what information about them, and their institutions, goes where. The Chatham House rule is an informal agreement created by the Chatham House membership organisation that states that information about a meeting is never attributed to the people who were at that meeting.

Rather, it remains behind closed doors. Gated communities keep the riff-raff out, so the people who can afford to live there can feel secure. Superinjunctions that prevent the media from reporting on something exist to keep the people who can afford the legal proceedings to create them out of the public eye: these are all the dominion of the elites. Meanwhile, it's the elites who have the power to manipulate our privacy to maintain social control.

The authors George Orwell and Aldous Huxley took this to the extreme in the dystopias of *1984* and *Brave New World*. In both novels, the majority's individual rights have been eradicated for the supposed benefit of all, but the ruling classes always seem to have a little pocket of secrecy where they can hide. The further up the ladder you go, the more you're able to keep from everyone else. The rationales behind both these fictional systems, and indeed modern phenomena such as the upsurge of CCTV cameras on UK streets, is to create a society that believes it is constantly being watched. Social control is enforced by freaking everyone out.

In 1787, the philosopher Jeremy Bentham described a blueprint for exactly this system, but he called it the panopticon. It was a fictional prison, in which prisoners were unable to hide or communicate with anyone else, and believed they were being watched by an unseen guard. But the thing about it is that if you're inside there's no way to know when someone is watching – or indeed if anyone is. "The idea is to instil a self-discipline: you see yourself watched through another person's eyes," explains Dr Anja Steinbauer of the London School of Philosophy.

Dr Steinbauer believes the web is the ultimate example of the panopticon: "You don't need an architectural environment. We know, like the prisoners in the panopticon, that we might be being watched."

But while Bentham predicted the panopticon prison would constrain, correct or change our behaviour, it doesn't seem to be doing that online. We continue to dump private information into the online bin. We ignore the possibility that it will eventually come back to bite us. We forget that this information doesn't evaporate. Instead of evolving into a self-disciplined society, we are continually giving up more about ourselves, because everyone else does. It's just what you do online.

Of course we're worried about online privacy, said a study from 2009 from Ohio University, but we continue to upload enormous amounts of personal information to the web, and mostly to social networks and e-commerce. We are aware of privacy settings, but think that the benefits outweigh their concerns. They serve our needs and we are gratified. They are an indispensable part of many of our daily lives. With social networks, we have a place where we know we can connect with family, friends and colleagues, and have the tools to share photos of kids, parties, pets and holidays easily. We can also be sure that the people we are communicating with are who they say they are. In search engines, we get the answer to our queries. In e-commerce sites, we get the product we want, at an attractive price. But the privacy paradox, in which our attitudes say one thing but our behaviours say another, is more complicated than a cost-benefit analysis. As Yasmin Ibrahim from Queen Mary University in London says, the web that we use most often – social networks, search engines and e-commerce sites – are "conceptually designed" to reduce our concerns about privacy. The technologies themselves aren't passive. "These technologies are as neutral as guns," says Jim Adler, chief privacy officer and general manager of data systems at the information commerce firm Intelius.

There are indeed a few things that are psychologically unique about interacting via machines. First, we don't expect consequences. The web feels ephemeral, separate from so-called real life. What happens online stays online. That's totally untrue, of course. As we continue to intertwine our lives with technology, our virtual and physical selves evolve into the same beast, and therefore it's impossible to separate the consequences that affect one from the other. Something said or done in one place can easily be taken out of context and dropped into another. Ask the many people who've been fired from their jobs for posting party pictures on their Facebook timelines.

Second, according to the Ohio study, online we experience an extreme version of the so-called "third person effect": we rationalise, through our infernal, eternal human nature, that if something's going to go wrong, it'll happen to the other guy. So we won't change our privacy settings on a social network or turn off cookies on our browsers to keep the details of our surfing away from advertisers: only when we experience a personal violation will we be more careful to protect ourselves and our information.

Third, we're unable to imagine the vastness of the potential audience we communicate with when we're online, so we treat the computer like a confidant, a confessor. We have an intimate relationship with our computer terminals; our laptops, mobile phones, desktops and tablets feel private, and the networks we hang out in feel closed. In order to make a connection with others, we feel it's OK to share private information. "We think the web is a kind of conversation," explains Dr Kieran O'Hara, a philosopher and web scientist at the University of Southampton. "It feels a bit like writing letters, a bit like a telephone conversation. But it's all that and much more."

So why do we share so much? To compensate for an environment that is stripped of natural, interpersonal emotionality. We make it fertile through our psychological commitment to a social space that really exists only in our minds. We spend most of our time online looking for rich connections in a lean space, so we divulge more in order to find similarities with other people. We help the virtual world grow by planting little bits of humanity for other people to see and to connect with. Lane DiNicola believes our desire to keep things to ourselves is actually anathema to a functioning social environment: "A lot of definitions of culture itself will say that it's about sharing: the exchange of ideas, ways of doing things, material artefacts. The whole idea of privacy and maintaining privacy runs counter to a cultural drive."

The machines get a whole lot of intimate information too, and this lives in databases where complicated pattern-matching and cross-referencing routines expose connections that would otherwise have remained invisible. That's why it was possible for Facebook to have on record the personal email addresses that Max Schrems never divulged himself. At its heart, the web is a connection engine. It has the uncanny, inhuman power to bring stuff that might not appear relevant or interesting to the attention of people who would find it valuable. As Dr O'Hara puts it, "The main protection of our privacy has not been that the information is not there or hasn't been kept; it's that you can't find the information easily." Legally, this is called "practical obscurity". Charles Dickens described exactly this in his novel *Bleak House*, published in 1853. O'Hara explains: "There's a family scandal, there's some information that will reveal the family scandal; the information is in the public domain, but the guy who holds the information can't read, so he is simply unable to make the connections." But information that may not have been accessible in the past can now be obtained in roundabout ways. The magic machine could eradicate practical obscurity.

The computerised systems that are used to make sense of the information that we leave behind us are starting to make ever more sophisticated connections and learn patterns. Some people view this as a chance to observe behaviours in real time, draw real-time conclusions and effect real-time change. They can be used to identify outbreaks of contagious diseases, for example, and intervene before they spread further. The health community is starting to do what it calls digital epidemiology: "Digital data sources, when harnessed appropriately, can provide local and timely information about disease and health dynamics in populations around the world," explained a consortium of researchers from the Centre for Infectious Disease Dynamics and the Department of Biology at Penn State University, the Department of Public Health Sciences at Karolinska Institutet in Stockholm, Harvard School of Public Health, the US National Institutes of Health and the College of Computer and Information Sciences at Northeastern University in 2012.

Although computational power of the machine can produce impressive and valuable results, it can also deliver data that leads to conclusions that absolutely demand a human being – who can distinguish things that someone may wish to keep private – to interpret it. In early 2012, a 15-year-old girl's shopping behaviour at US chain Target told the system that she was pregnant. It automatically printed and sent coupons for maternity wear and baby toys to her home, where she still lived with her parents. She hadn't told them the news, but the superstore did it for her.

The place I currently call home is one of the most fiercely observed cities in the world. London is studded with CCTV cameras, capturing an estimated 70–300 images of each resident every day. In Newham,

London, the council even trialled facial recognition software in their CCTV cameras to develop dossiers on its residents' patterns of activity. On top of that, digital public infrastructure – speed cameras, travel cards, wireless toll payments – knows what our movements are credit card companies know what we buy; and our mobile phone operators have details of who we phone and when.

It could be even worse. In early 2012, the UK government proposed a draft Communications Data Bill that would effectively create a giant database of all internet activity that happened within its boundaries. They outlined a plan to use the data, held by an undetermined organisation for an undefined period of time, to look for patterns of potential terrorist activity. The proposed legislation is currently technologically impossible; it would require a storage system the size of Wales to capture the data that would be collected every day. Yet when word got out about the so-called "snooping bill", it caused a public stink about how much digital information is collected, and who, ultimately, is in charge of it.

Collectively, this is known as "Big Data". That's data that's too big to compute easily, yet is so rich that it is being used by institutions with enough computational power at hand in both the public and the private sectors to identify what people want before they are even aware they want it. Big Data poses an enormous threat to our civil liberties because it gives a disproportionate amount of control to machines. "Given enough data, intelligence and power, corporations and government can connect dots in ways that only previously existed in science fiction," says Alexander Howard from technology publisher O'Reilly Media. To give one example, in 2010, an experimental system called Pax was developed to identify where in the world uprisings might occur based on what people are searching for on Google on their computers or on their Android operating system mobile phones. When a place is identified as potentially "in trouble", the team would write a report and circulate it to NGOs, journalists, governments and interested others who are based there. This ambitious project was supported by Google, and its steering group included a professor of war studies at King's College London, the former chief executive of Channel 5 and the director of communications of the United Nations.

What's wrong with a system like Pax? Well, web searches can certainly give away a lot of valuable information about us and what we want: the Google advertising model – a system that has revolutionised the industry – is based on the idea that what we do online reflects our intentions. That's why when we search for dog food, we'll see ads for pet supplies on other websites, and when we log on to Gmail to tell a friend about plans for Friday night, we'll see ads about local hotspots. So, sure, if a large number of searches in a particular geographical location include the words "indicating aggression", as the creators of Pax put it, that could suggest that something is about to kick off. But it could also implicate innocent people who happen to be looking for similar keywords at the same time. The word "plot", for example, could refer to a terrorist plot or a garden plot.

But surely it's impossible to track down a person based only on their search terms? Well, no. In 2006, two *New York Times* technology reporters found Thelma Arnold, a 62-year-old woman from Lilburn, Georgia who was revealed to be "AOL Searcher No. 4417749", based only on three months' worth of search terms. They found her home address and phone number and a whole lot of other intelligence using search strings like "numb fingers", "dog that urinates on everything" and "landscapes in Lilburn, Georgia". "Data can say quite a lot," says

Alexander Howard. "One has to be very careful to verify quality and balance it with human expertise and intuition."

The most important thing for the organisations that have the databases in the Big Data age is the kind of information they have access to. You can have a database filled to the brim with potentially valuable disease data that's missing a crucial demographic detail that makes it usable. You can have access to the kind of information Facebook kept about Schrems, but if you don't have his name, or the names of the people he's connected to, you can only draw so many useful conclusions before you run into a virtual brick wall. Digital services, from social networks to smartphone apps, all keep different kinds of things about us. But, most of our web activity is fragmented: it's not in one convenient bin but in multiple accounts that we create or that are created about us by services that watch us as we traverse the web. An easy way to get some idea of just how valuable the data held by any single web service is, is to look at the price paid when the service changes hands. Surprising amounts suggest it has collected important information about you.

In early 2012, Facebook spent $1 billion on a smartphone photo-sharing service called Instagram. Many people were flabbergasted to find that a piece of software that puts coloured filters on snapshots was so valuable to the world's biggest social network, especially since that service was less than a year old. But it becomes less surprising when you know how Facebook defines identity and how Instagram connects its users to one another and to the rest of the web.

Facebook thinks identity is made of three things: real names, social connections (preferably reciprocated) and photographs. Instagram clearly ticks the photographs box, but Facebook already has its own photo-sharing system, so why all the fuss? Although Instagram users don't have to use their real names, the app becomes much more useful if it's connected to other social networks such as Twitter, Flickr and Tumblr, where people register with their real names and email addresses, and where they may be connected with people other than those whom they have as friends on Facebook. So what Facebook got, ultimately, for the $1 billion was a whole lot of new information about its users and their relationships, plus a whole lot of useful stuff from people who may not use Facebook themselves. Obtaining the details of the people they've not been able to access before is worth a fortune to them.

Even before Instagram, Facebook's data was enormously rich. As far back as 2006 chief executive Mark Zuckerberg bragged to author David Kirkpatrick that he could predict when you'd split up with a romantic partner and who you'd date next based on whose wall you posted on and what you said there. Police departments long ago realised that Facebook connections can provide the missing link in their search for criminals. One evening in 2006, college student Marc Chiles decided that he needed to empty his bladder between pubs. Rather than look for a loo, he relieved himself outside a fraternity house. This is illegal in the US state of Illinois. While Chiles managed to escape the scene of the crime as the cops pulled up, another member of his party wasn't so lucky. The police had a conversation with another student named Adam Gartner, who claimed not to know Chiles. During a phone call Gartner received while being questioned, the police were able to identify the name of the guy who peed in the bush. In an attempt to tie the two together, they asked Gartner to log into a new social network that was sweeping the college circuit at the time. Unluckily for Gartner, not only was Chiles listed as one of his Facebook friends, but there were also loads of photos of the pair of them on his "wall". Chiles was fined $145 for public urination; Gartner was fined $195 for obstruction of justice. Oops. Seven years on, a Facebook search is part of many police departments' standard investigation processes. The NYPD, for example, now compares Facebook profiles, uploads and relationships with its own face recognition software, and has used it to arrest and prosecute criminals for offences as severe as attempted murder.

Even if you're not planning a crime spree, friends' online activities can expose things about you that you'd rather keep quiet. "Your friends will become if not the biggest danger, the biggest source of information," warns Dr Kieran O'Hara. "They will provide much more information about you that is much more personal." Your friends are the ones who will drop information bombs about significant others and where you were last night, as well as revealing details of your birthdays, anniversaries and where you go on holiday.

In March 2012, the US supermarket chain Walmart bought the startup Social Calendar, one of the most popular calendar services on Facebook. At that time, Social Calendar had more than 15 million registered users, offering them an easy way to record special events, birthdays and anniversaries, backed up with automated email and SMS reminders. At the time of the purchase, Social Calendar already had over 110 million personal notifications in its databases. From the perspective of a retailer, this information is gold dust, revealing when you are going on holiday (do you need sunscreen or a woolly hat?), when you might want a present for your mum's birthday, and when the anniversary of a loved one's death is approaching.

On the face of it, what the acquisition meant for Social Calendar's users was that Walmart could create even more complete profiles for them by cross-referencing the service's information with the retailer's own data, including any purchasing history and patterns, and any other databases it has access to. In many countries, this includes government and medical records. The Social Calendar purchase also eroded the privacy of those who had never agreed to be part of that world in the first place, but were listed in its users' reminders. People who had never signed up for the Social Calendar app, and even those who had shunned Facebook completely, had a little piece of them bought by Walmart. With a little digging, the superstore would now be able to find out when your technophobic grandma's birthday was. And if she had ever shopped at Walmart, this little – but valuable – detail could now be added to her permanent record.

When a Social Calendar user listed a friend's birthday or the details of a holiday to Malaga, she or he probably had no idea that information would end up in the hands of a US supermarket. And when someone searches for something online, shares photos with friends on a social network, or even just surfs around, they don't think this information will be stored, cross-referenced and sold to the highest bidder. "People give out their data often without thinking about it," says Viviane Reding, the European Commission's vice-chancellor for justice, fundamental rights and citizenship. "They have no idea that it will be sold to third parties." Users continue to populate databases with increasingly valuable personal information that, as commercial property, can be transferred to a new company with a different privacy ethos. Such is the nature of mergers and acquisitions. The only indication users have when something changes is an updated privacy policy or more personalised ads on websites. We have no say in the matter at all.

Our expectations of privacy, then, have not yet caught up with reality. "When I grew up in Greensborough, Alabama, the population was 1,200," says Intelius's Jim Adler. "If you cut school, everyone knew it by dinner." But many of us migrated to urban environments and experienced a kind of practical obscurity. The urbanisation movement from village to city has meant that we have developed a sense that we can be anonymous, lost in the crowd.

The sense of anonymity extends online, but the difference is that no one, unless they use tools specifically designed for this purpose, is actually untraceable.

Things become even more complicated when the users of software systems and architectures come from around the world but privacy expectations reflect the service's American roots.

This was particularly apparent in Max Schrems' case against Facebook. Soon after he received his dossier, Schrems began campaigning against the social network, trying to inspire the company to take on transparency, and to force it to adhere to European law. He set up a site called Europe vs Facebook, with information about his dossier and how other people could get theirs. "Our expectations of privacy in the US versus Europe are very different," says Adler. "We are currently negotiating which is more important: the rights of the individual or the rights of knowledge."

In 2012, Facebook conceded and began complying with a European data privacy law about storage of personal information. The company now deletes anything typed into its search field within six months, and most of the rest within one year. But this isn't enough for some, including the European Commission's Viviane Reding. In the EU, she has campaigned for the "right to be forgotten", extending the existing EU's 1995 Data Protection Directive, which establishes by law that private data is the property of the individual and that she or he has a right to request that any information about themselves is deleted at any time. "More and more people feel uncomfortable about being traced everywhere, about a brave new world," she said. This "private" data includes everything uploaded to social networks and search histories, as well as details of mobile phone calls, usage of "frequent buyer" store cards and itemised credit card bills. Unsurprisingly, information held by public bodies remains exempt. But will the right to be forgotten change anything? One of the problems with such top-down systems is that it's almost impossible to track down every little piece of you that's been added to a database and request that it is removed. "The digital traces we want to leave are accompanied by digital traces we don't want to leave," says O'Hara. It's likely that, even if you delete all the data you can find, some digital shadow will remain.

With each new communication technology, we are forced to renegotiate our personal and social boundaries about what is and what isn't private, because each new technology exposes us in a different way. We're already undergoing this process with the web, adapting to our virtual environment and what we put online. It may be that everyone must undergo the humiliation of having themselves misrepresented online, as something that's published in one context is co-opted for another. It may be that our digital shadows will become our marks of trust and reliability; to have none will be a sign that we have something we're ashamed of, something to hide.

We won't know how this will affect our future selves until we collectively decide how to cope with the way the technology collects little pieces of us and connects our lives. The web forces us to recognise that, although we think we do, we have no control over the information that's already out there.

GRASSROOTS POLITICS, GLOBAL REVOLUTION

On 25 December 1990, the most radical innovation of modern times was released to the public. In a quiet computer lab at CERN in Geneva, Sir Tim Berners-Lee switched on the world wide web. This simple act set the stage for the transformation of political power, global economics, social interactions and personal identity. "Tim Berners-Lee created a new mode of human communication," said Stephen Fry when I spoke with him for the BBC Two series *The Virtual Revolution* in 2009. "He created a new way of allowing communication to work in extraordinarily connected ways." Well-known for his passion for technology, the comedian reflected on what the web meant to him when he discovered it almost two decades before. "It seemed like a great new world. It seemed like a new democracy. It seemed like a new way of people coming together and spreading news, of educating, of giving yourselves information and access to people and cultures and history. It seemed the most fantastic, radical and extraordinary development since Gutenberg produced his Bible."

Like the printing press that printed that first bible, the web has been credited with ushering in an enlightenment: the power of information is now in the hands of the people, and, if you listen to the hype, our social, psychological and cognitive capabilities are ascending to levels of sophistication that humanity has never before witnessed. With the web we can galvanise, coordinate, collaborate and overthrow. The web, they say, is the most powerful harbinger of social change.

But is it really? The political upheavals in North Africa at the beginning of 2011 that are now known as the Arab Spring were described at the time as Facebook and Twitter revolutions, but something was already brewing and would likely have bubbled over even without the web. Barack Obama's election to the US presidency in 2008 was called the first internet election, but more money was raised for his campaign via telephone. How big a part has the web really played in these sweeping social changes? More importantly, are we really feeling its revolutionary effects at a personal level? Are autocracies really threatened by computer systems? Are we on the way to abolishing social inequalities?

In 2003, a crop of publishing platforms, like LiveJournal, Blogger and MySpace, became part of a new era in the history of the web. Technology publisher and pundit Tim O'Reilly called services like these, "Web 2.0", implying a totally new way to interact with the internet. Before this so-called social media surge, it was tough to publish anything online without some knowledge of computer programming. But after 2003, new services gave people the right tools to publish quickly and easily without the need to learn programming. Millions since have been able to grab virtual megaphones, and quickly and easily share their revolutionary ideas.

Over the last two decades, there has been a change in the way we view access to information: many now assume it's a basic human right. Authoritarian regimes have tried to clamp down on dissident websites, but almost instantly work-arounds open up the pipelines again. The way the internet is built means, simply, that it cannot be shut down: there is no one central waypoint that all information goes through. If one route seems blocked, the computer system will try another one, and another, and another until it finds its destination.

In Yemen, for example, former journalist and computer programmer Walid Al-Saqaf developed an encryption technology called alkasir, which allows people to circumvent government censorship. As the son of a journalist murdered for reporting on a corrupt government, Al-Saqaf wanted to use his skills to get around a blockade implemented by the Yemeni government, "because I felt it would have been a betrayal to my own profession to simply manipulate what people see." He runs a news site, YemeniPortal.net, that publishes news articles from non-government sources, and therefore people within the country can't access it. By using alkasir, however, they can see his site because the software hides where in the world they're from. "Information freedom is essential if you're really going to live a dignified life," he argues. He believes that presenting his audience with both government and dissident news sources will allow them to take better decisions.

China is perhaps the most infamous web censor, but there is evidence that even its Great Firewall, which doesn't allow people within the country to access foreign news, news that criticises the government and some services like Facebook, is being relaxed. The country's most popular blogger is Han Han, a 28-year-old professional rally car driver and author. He posts treatises that are openly critical of the current Chinese government, talking about party corruption and instability, yet, because he speaks in the vernacular of the youth audience and has a tremendous following, his personal politics are generally overlooked by the censors.

"Although the internet is [still] controlled, when compared with traditional media it better reflects reality," Han says. People are able to create symbols of resistance using photographs or phrases that represent content that the government usually bans. "The atmosphere is not as terrifying as people in some Western countries may think," he says. "This is a game, and I'm playing by other people's rules. I don't think that the government disagrees with the ideas in the articles that were censored; they are afraid of the ideas spreading."

The crowd has indeed become a powerful force in the battle against the repression of information. The next generation of technologists are using the web's hyper-connectivity and plug-and-play capabilities to crowdsource action. In Kenya, activist Ory Okolloh released Ushahidi, a tool that gathers streams of information generated by eyewitnesses reporting in via their mobile phones and displays it on a Google Map. During the post-election violence in 2008, it was used to identify active hubs of resistance, and to share news about what was happening on the ground from people who were actually there. The technology circumvented traditional hierarchies and communicated what was happening – live – to people inside and outside the country, despite government attempts to block traditional media during the conflict.

Despite all of this, old media such as television and newspapers cannot be totally discounted. Tom Steinberg is the founder and director of MySociety, a British technology company that builds services to connect individuals, local communities and local government. Steinberg argues that there are two ways in which politics has been transformed by the web: "partisan campaigning to exert power and to beat your opponents into a pulp; and the creation of what you might call empowering platforms using general-purpose tools that let people communicate, act, exert power or achieve goals like requesting information out of the government."

MySociety's most successful projects, TheyWorkForYou, FixMyStreet and No 10 Petitions, have inspired people to get involved. "The internet presents more opportunity to lower these barriers," Steinberg says.

"You can make things that say, 'Go on, just have a go'." Steinberg likes
to think that his tools support a vibrant, healthy and lively democracy
("a rude and obnoxious place"), encouraging communities of voices
loud enough to be heard by political bodies. He is pleased when people
use what he has developed to demand radical change. Yet when it
comes to "politics with a capital P", like Barack Obama's strategy in
the 2008 US presidential elections, he recognises the importance of
old media formats. "If I was running an election campaign and I had
£10,000, I would still spend it all on TV adverts, leaflets and posters.
The internet is good at all sorts of things, but shoving your message
down the throats of people who don't care – which is what it takes to
spike campaigns and win – it's not particularly great at."

The web has transformed the amount of information we have at our
fingertips. Everyone has the freedom to contribute to and access the
overwhelming library of knowledge online. Those who have historically
controlled distribution, like governments, the clergy, the elites and the
press, are having to reposition themselves in the face of this tsunami
of information. "Individuals without great wealth or bases of power
and the industrial world economy can exert influence on others who
find their ideas resonating with them," explained US Vice President
Al Gore when interviewed for *The Virtual Revolution*. "It is inherently
democratising and egalitarian and promotes a greater role for the rule
of reason."

Social change isn't just about access to information, however;
it's about choosing which cause to get behind. And while political
revolutions get headlines, there are many organisations that try to
make a difference in people's lives closer to home. The web is a
remarkable publishing platform for charities with little or no cash.

"Digital tools and platforms are becoming the key channel to the public to encourage fundraising, action taking or general awareness," says Karina Brisby, head of interactive campaigns for the poverty charity Oxfam. Indeed, the online world is full of Twitter feeds excitedly documenting actions, blogs dutifully updated with shaky videos and Facebook pages asking you to click and show your support. But if the outcome they want is a pot of gold, charities will be disappointed: the trend from a decade of research published in the *International Journal of Nonprofit and Voluntary Sector Marketing* shows that the web is best used as a communication tool, not for fundraising. In other words, it's just as tough to get people to put their hands in their pockets online as off. In some ways, the donation drives at the office were more effective, because it was more difficult to ignore a colleague shaking a collection tin at your desk than one sending a link to a donation page.

This said, the web can only reflect the experiences of the people who use it, and in the reflection are other prejudices and injustices. There are more than ten million people living in the UK with a long-term illness, impairment or physical disability, according to the Office for Disability Issues, and although medical treatment and pre-birth screening has reduced this number dramatically over the last half-century, many of the problems faced by those affected have not changed. Compared with their non-disabled counterparts, they are still more likely to be poor and unemployed with fewer qualifications, more likely to be the victims of crime, and more likely to experience occupational and social discrimination. This was supposed to have been fixed by the web. After all, crudely, there are no physical barriers online. If you believe the utopians, the web should be a totally accessible resource where everyone can achieve personal and social self-actualisation. It should be the great leveller. It should be, but, as always, it's more complicated than that.

In 2003, I started an MSc in social psychology, with all of the wide-eyed innocence of someone who'd just discovered the web: I was going to prove beyond a shadow of a doubt that it could revolutionise society. I interviewed people who had injured their spinal cords so severely that they were almost completely paralysed. I figured that physical disability becomes unimportant in cyberspace with the right tools and, thanks to some exceptional engineering adaptations, the people who participated in this research were able to play some incredibly mechanically complicated games through fully able-bodied online personas, exercising psychological selves rather than physical ones. Two results stood out. First, the web offered personal and physical anonymity to a population that experiences a significant amount of stigma elsewhere. In general, it allows people who cannot "pass" in real-world situations – like the people who took part in the study – to be unrestricted, physically. It transforms the power dynamics that bubble under (and occasionally over) the surface in a society when a disability is apparent.

Second, the people in the study described the web as an empowering platform, giving them the sense that they were in charge of their own destinies. This "levelling up" doesn't just happen in games: getting information, collecting a posse, being an agent of change through whatever means gives the individual an ego boost, and is far more achievable now than it ever has been.

I was surprised how little research had been carried out, given the potential social benefit. Almost universally, the results of the few small studies that have been published in this area show that the web is an untapped resource for disabled people, with the potential to transform social participation by providing information and networks. Based on these, there are countless initiatives to get people with disabilities online.

Unfortunately, this is part of the problem. All of this condones a philosophy called the Social Model of Disability, which says that it's society that creates the barriers to access and equality that people with disabilities experience, rather than the disability itself. In other words, it's architecture, culture and social constraints that exclude disabled people from full participation. Clearly, the web has been a great place to test this: remove the obvious barriers and the evidence uncovers happy, fully-functioning members of society. But these barriers still exist. We still live in the real world. One of the strongest criticisms against the Social Model is that by hiding a physical disability, or attributing non-physical impairments to clumsiness or inattention, disabled people perpetuate a discriminatory society and reinforce the perceptions of personal tragedy, inefficacy and stigma. The web is the greatest passing platform of all: everyone is "normal" online. Meanwhile, what is happening to our attitudes towards disability offline?

Over the past decade, there have been improvements for people with disabilities in employment, education and participation in cultural activities, but the web is not the only factor in this change. Unsurprisingly, the gaps between disabled and non-disabled people in these areas are still significant; the UK government's Office for Disability Issues reports that only 48% of disabled adults are employed, compared with 78% of the able-bodied.

If the web's limitless potential for social change was actually being realised, we would expect greater transformation at the individual level to have happened over the last 20 years. But as we continue to populate this technological tabula rasa, we bring offline social hierarchies to the online world. It may be a technology that can, if used correctly, topple injustice, but first we must recognise injustice before we even try.

MISINFORMATION, DISINFORMATION AND THE PRESS

For Peter Beaumont, the *Observer*'s foreign affairs correspondent, the revolution in Egypt revealed more than the power of the people to triumph over repressive regimes; it also taught him something about his own profession. Beaumont trained as a journalist pre-web, but has adopted the new technologies in his news-gathering techniques. When the rioters took to Tahir Square in Cairo in Egypt in early 2011 to ultimately overthrow the Mubarak regime, of course he and his team were on the ground. But reporting from the front line of this conflict was a step back in time. The dictator had effectively turned off the internet by forcing the four primary internet providers to stop data traffic into and out of the country. "We went back to what we used to do: write up the story on the computer, go to the business centre and print it out, and dictate it over the phone," he told me afterwards. "In Egypt, we didn't have to worry about what was on the internet; we just had to worry about what we were seeing. It was absolutely liberating."

The web's effect on news reporting is considered clear evidence that it is a revolutionary technology: news editors and, in some cases, the governments they serve, are no longer the gatekeepers to information because the cost of distribution has almost completely disappeared. In effect, everyone now has his or her own printing press.

As consumers, we are now able to find enormous amounts of different types of information about stories. Emily Bell, director of the

Tow Center for Digital Journalism at Columbia University and former editor of Guardian Unlimited, points at the coverage of the attacks on the World Trade Center on September 11, 2001 as the global incident that foreshadowed how events are covered today. "Linear TV just could not deliver," she says. "People used the web to connect to the experience by watching it in real time on TV, through message boards and forums. They posted bits of information they knew themselves and aggregated it with links from elsewhere. For most, the delivery was crude, but the reporting, linking and sharing nature of news coverage emerged at that moment."

This mutualised model of news reporting, promoted by *Guardian* editor Alan Rusbridger, recognises the important and very modern relationship between the news consumer and the professional journalist when it comes to gathering stories. Yet, for the reporters on the ground in Egypt who were trading without the web, the greatest frustration was not that they were disconnected from the network that provided the context, but that they struggled to get their stories out. Beaumont, meanwhile, found it a relief. "The way [Egypt] was reported didn't have all the ifs and buts coming from looking over your shoulder to try to figure out what the world is doing at the moment, or who's saying what. You just had the news, and the news was happening right in front of you."

Reporters love the web for its multiplicity of perspectives and the library of knowledge that provides the context for stories. Paul Mason, economics editor for the BBC's *Newsnight* programme, says he uses the web to help him judge what's happening and what's important. "If you are following ten key economists on Twitter and some very intelligent blogs, you can quickly get to where you need to be: the stomach-churning question, 'OK, what do I do to move this story on?'" Bell, however, warns that journalists must not get too carried away with tools like Facebook and Twitter: "Understanding what is better done by automated techniques, what is better done by networks of witnesses, and where professional journalism actually adds value is key to understanding how news gathering must adapt to cope with the web."

Sometimes the professional thing is to ignore the web altogether. In 2010, CNN found itself in a public mess when it tried to break a story first based only on the "Twitter line" that a US doctor shot several soldiers in the Fort Hood military base in Texas. An "eyewitness", Tearah Moore, was tweeting from within the compound, publishing updates and photographs. The news outlet published these, reporting inaccurate information – that there were several shooters and that the main suspect had been killed – and the media organisation ultimately had to retract its reports.

On 7 December 2011, the *Guardian* released an interactive image that described how rumour and misinformation spread online. It was part of the new trend in investigative reporting, "data journalism". It pulls newsworthy trends out of large amounts of data, and often represents the information in easy-to-understand graphics that readers can poke at to drill down into more detail. One of its most popular articles in its *Reading the Riots* series (covering the violence which took place in England in August of the same year) tracked the Twitter accounts that had initially tweeted what eventually turned out to be false information, and how that spread like wildfire on the social network. These were the people who convinced a surprising number of logical thinkers who were bamboozled by the chaos on the streets that a tiger had escaped London Zoo or that the London Eye ferris wheel had been set on fire by rioters. Stories like these ricocheted around the Twitterverse over the four days of the riots, and certain individuals emerged as ringleaders in the imaginings of unlikely events. Because people were looking for information and these stories were plausible enough, they were picked up and shared via social media, spreading like wildfire over the network. The individuals in question were identified on the news site by their Twitter handles, exposing them as sources of false information.

"First-hand witnesses cannot see the big picture," says Yves Eudes, a reporter with the French newspaper *Le Monde*. "They're not trained to understand if what they're seeing is relevant to the big picture, or to see what really happens. They're trained to see what they want to see. If you only rely on Twitter or Facebook, you might end up howling with the wolves." And in the case of the story of the England riots and the tiger from London Zoo, this is exactly what happened.

Eudes's caution does not mean he discounts the value of the tools that the web offers citizen journalists; *Le Monde* was one of the papers, along with the *Guardian* and the *New York Times*, that worked with Julian Assange to publish the WikiLeaks cables in 2011. "The WikiLeaks team very quickly realised they didn't have the resources to exploit all this material – to analyse and publish it – and they didn't have the credibility. So they really needed people like ourselves. It was an odd couple, but they needed us as much as we needed them [...] Suddenly we have all these new competitors which, if they're bold and well-organised, can change the course of news worldwide in a way that was completely unthinkable before the internet."

Emily Bell views the WikiLeaks story as a milestone in modern journalism, but believes that it will have less impact on the future of news gathering than the coverage of September 11. "WikiLeaks was an event which clarified how the world of journalism had changed, without actually necessarily changing it itself," she says.

Ultimately, the fundamentals of news gathering have not been transformed by the web: "I need to know how to write or take a photo, and I need to be good at analysis," says Eudes. "Learning how to use tools is different from saying everyone is a reporter. Anyone can make bread, but it's lousy bread. You need to spend time like a true, professional baker to learn to make good bread."

Although for *Newsnight*'s Mason the public can help shape a story through their first-hand accounts, he believes it is crucial that print and TV journalists break away from their web connections to be on the ground. "It was gratifying to see so many foreign correspondents suddenly turn up in Egypt and interface with reality," he says. For Beaumont, working from Tahir Square without the web was a reminder of a purer form of journalism. "You forget that the internet, for all its great advantages, is an incredible distraction," he says. "You're always questioning yourself about whether what you're reading by other people matches what you're witnessing yourself. If you don't have to worry about that, you can just concentrate on pure observational reporting. Which is a pleasure."

CONSULTING DR WEB

A doctor dies and goes to heaven. When he arrives at the Pearly Gates in his scrubs, he strides up to the front of the queue and demands to be let in because he clearly deserves special treatment. After all, he's been through medical school. He can save lives. He is, in short, a doctor.

Saint Peter isn't impressed. He sends him to the back of the queue to wait with everyone else. Moments later, another guy, also wearing surgical scrubs, walks to the front and the gates swing open for him. The first doctor storms back up to Saint Peter and demands to know why he let the other one in. Saint Peter responds, "Oh, that's God. He thinks he's a doctor."

It is a terrible generalisation, I know, but the stereotype of doctors is that they think they have all the answers. And when it comes to matters of the heart, lungs, liver, pancreas and other cuts of the human corpus, they certainly know more than the average Joe or Jane. But the tide is turning, thanks to the web. The public are increasingly informed about their medical options and personal wellbeing, and they're beginning to question the medicine man's authority. Not only is anything you want to know about any symptom or lifestyle choice available online in triplicate, but that information frequently comes with prognoses, treatments and social support networks, all of it of varying in degrees of accuracy or helpfulness. You can now bypass the doctor's surgery completely by self-diagnosing and self-medicating. You can find out all you want or need to know about the experience of having an ailment by logging into a health-related community. The web has managed to

UNTANGLING THE WEB

topple the traditional hierarchy of expertise that's based on years of experience and stacks of diplomas and specialist knowhow, by giving everyone just enough information to make us dangerous.

This may not be wise. At the beginning of 2011, a report released by UK healthcare organisation BUPA and the London School of Economics overwhelmingly condemned online health information, and us for believing in it. According to the report, more people than ever before are using the web to find out about ailments before or instead of visiting the doctor. Our access to medical knowledge is unprecedented, and we have begun to feel an incredible control over our wellbeing and how to maintain it. Alarmingly, however, only a quarter of the 12,000 people who were surveyed checked the reliability of information they found online. Very few looked at where it came from, or whether it was still relevant. After all, the information that you found via Dr Google has no sell-by date and the information might be based on invalid clinical trials or even hearsay. It could have been commercially motivated and therefore totally biased, but people believed it because it was what they were looking for.

BUPA and LSE found that, in the modern web-enabled age, a typical medical consultation follows this trajectory: 1) you discover a growth, 2) you do a Google search, 3) you believe the first result that confirms your expectations. This isn't hyperbole. In 2008, the Pew Internet & American Life Project reported that most people in the US below the age of 50 started "a typical health information session" with a search engine: three-quarters of people aged between 18 and 29 and 65% of people aged between 30 and 49 did. The people who were aged 50 or above were more likely to start at specialist websites and work themselves into a tizzy from there. All of this searching assumes that they knew what they were supposed to be looking for in the first place.

The role of the search engine in mediating our health care is nothing to be sniffed at: the Pew report said their survey respondents most often only looked at two websites when they were searching for medical advice, and the top three results served up by Google were most likely to be the first ports of call. Google is now a particularly important doorway to our physical and mental wellbeing. We have "a remarkable sense of confidence and trust in search engines," said Pew's authors. The search engine doesn't consider the searcher's age, gender, general health status or pre-existing conditions. It just spits out the worst-case scenario. And you, the lay person with the pounding head or the pounding chest, are left to cope.

It is absolutely possible to descend into a rabbit hole of self-diagnostic misinformation because of the way the web allows people to seek until they find the information that suits them. The Microsoft researchers found that a search for "headache" is as likely to suggest "brain tumour" as the cause as "caffeine withdrawal". The annual incidence of brain tumours in the US, where this study was based (although it used the global web as its data pool) is one in 10,000. And a search for "chest pain"? You'll more likely discover you're going to have a heart attack than either indigestion or heartburn. Which is, of course, ridiculous. But don't take my word for it. Get a second opinion: that's according to a study by Microsoft Research in 2008.

This is the most common ailment that can be caught online. It also strikes medical students around their second year, when they're starting to get into the nitty-gritty of pathologies. I had a version of this so-called medical student syndrome when I was taking my psychopathology courses: looking at all the symptoms of all the mental disorders listed in the American Psychiatric Association's diagnostic bible, the *DSM-IV*, it was clear that not only was I a paranoid schizophrenic, but all of my close friends and family most certainly had PTSD, OCD, borderline personality disorder, narcissistic personality disorder, Münchausen syndrome or a combination of all of the above. "Cyberchondria", according to Microsoft's Ryen White and Eric Horovitz, can cause a significant amount of anxiety among previously non-anxious individuals as they apply the little information that they have to their particular circumstances. Yes, online medical advice can be frightening. It can also leave us feeling overwhelmed by too much information.

Of course, anyone with an interest in their health pre-web could have gone to the library and incorrectly self-diagnosed with a basic understanding of the Dewey Decimal System and the help of research journals and diagnostic manuals, but nowadays a search engine will deliver exactly what's wrong in a nice, printable format. Social networks and forums will add evidence and provide support, as well as offer a whole database of new tics and symptoms that you may not have realised you should have, if you do actually have that ailment. Armed with your printout, a dose of false certainty and more than a spoonful of paranoia, you march to your medical practitioner and demand treatment. The problem is that the potentially questionable information you've received from a search can cause you to over-emphasise symptoms at the doctor's office, leading to an incorrect diagnosis.

It's not just at the doctor's office where this cyberchondria presents itself. Some online support communities normalise symptoms, leading to often very self-destructive, unhealthy behaviour. The best-known known example of this is the pro-ana community, which exacerbates the eating disorder anorexia nervosa by giving its members a place to share anything from tips and tricks for hiding weight loss from loved ones or doctors to "thinspiration" photos of emaciated women. Pro-ana sites proliferated with the web, particularly after *The Oprah*

Winfrey Show aired a feature in 2001, despite attempts to block them or to counteract them with pro-recovery sites that try to help people suffering from the mental illness work towards health. But banning them doesn't do any good: the community just went underground and became more discreet. The information is still out there on the other side of a Google search. You just have to know what to look for.

So, yes, the web is changing how we think about our health and what we do when something goes wrong. When it was still in its infancy, the medical community expected that doctors' paternalistic approach – you have ailment X and you can only fix it if you follow my advice – would evolve into a partnership in which they would help a patient move towards recovery rather than prescribe it. What has actually happened is that we've developed a way to negotiate between the experts who know quite a bit, and the people who do not know a lot but think they do. Doctors now have to persuade their patients that they offer the best counsel, not Dr Web.

After watching this evolve over twenty years, doctors and support groups are moving online to take the weight off most of the basic complaints and ailments. In the UK, online and phone-based triage services have dramatically reduced the burden on GPs for illnesses that are easy to diagnose: at NHS Direct, 60% of the more than 350,000 web enquiries every month don't require a face-to-face appointment; the assessment, diagnosis and prescription happen online. For people who are time-strapped or who want to remain anonymous about their conditions, this is a welcome advance. And for patients and their families who want to know more about treatments that have been prescribed, the information from a credible source like the NHS provides peace of mind.

Obviously, the more information these kinds of services get from you about who you are and what your problem is, the better the advice.

But how much should we be willing to give? Websites will happily help identify what's wrong with you and recommend treatment if you submit your entire medical record, but should we maintain control over this potentially sensitive information? It's stored somewhere and used somehow – sometimes by medical professionals, at other times by corporations – and we have no idea what will happen to it in the future. A medical provider strapped for cash tomorrow may decide to sell the web records it collects today to a third-party insurance company, and today's 21-one-year-old with the awkward warts, no exercise regime, and a 40-a-day habit may ruin tomorrow's 34-four-year-old, granola eating, marathon runner's chance at getting a good health cover premium because of a past unhealthy lifestyle.

The wealth of information online has made us far better informed about our health, but we're not as well trained as the experts are to pick out what we should pay attention to. The value of health-related communities for psychological wellbeing and social support is also immense, but it, too, can send us into a spiral of self-fulfilling cyberchondria. Whether searching for information or giving it information about ourselves, we have a bad habit of putting our faith in the machine. A doctor who treats himself or herself is a fool. When it comes to our health, we should take heed of the input of the professionals. They really do know what they're talking about.

HOME IS WHERE THE HUB IS

According to the Office for National Statistics, 77% of households in the UK had an internet connection in 2011, and the government aims to get every house in the country connected with super-fast connections by 2015. We have no choice but to welcome the web into our homes, let it sit on our sofas and give it a cup of tea. And this has been a speedy infestation. As Michael Arnold put it in *The Connected Home*, "Homes were connected electronically to the outside world less than 100 years ago. And now the homes of many connect directly to friends, acquaintances, and [...] strangers: to the local community, to work, to social, political, and commercial organisations, to entertainment and service providers."

I am constantly connected to the web when I'm at home. I couldn't imagine life without it. It, as well as the things and people I connect to, is my companion when watching a movie, it is my entertainment system when I listen to the radio, it is my direct line to the family and friends I speak with on VoIP. Sociologists Kat Jungnickel and Genevieve Bell wouldn't think my over-networked experience is unusual. "Some read their emails and 'Google' for news in front of the TV whilst others breastfeed while surfing the net. In the kitchen, they look for recipes or talk with friends via IM. In bed they write emails or shop on eBay," they write in *Home is Where The Hub Is?* The rooms once allocated for particular things, like eating or sleeping, have been adopted by the web, and the many other things that it can do.

This requires a bit of control. Machines can creep, as one of Jungnickel and Bell's case studies describes: "Sal tells of the congestion zone caused by the chameleonic characteristics of the kitchen table," they write. "During the day it is her new computing space, and at night it is the social, cooking, washing-up space for both of them." Sounds complicated, and slightly dangerous. But when the world can be your workplace, and when a customer is able to enter your "shop" at any time of day or night, it can upset your work-life balance. "Broadly speaking," wrote Samuel Cameron and Mark Fox in the *Handbook on the Economics of Leisure* in 2012, "we expect work to have an atmosphere of work and home to have an atmosphere of home." People who work from home experience what Cameron and Fox call a "time elasticity illusion", particularly among others in the household who don't see why they can't do the hoovering or fix the leaky pipe in between answering emails. We must also contend with colleagues back in the office who think we spend all day in pyjamas watching TV. Cameron and Fox's work describes how our web-supported home-working has had an observable impact on leisure time. We become harder on ourselves, and employers keep a closer eye on our output. As the hours we work from home increase, employees report more rather than less work-related stress. After all, it's still a job and things have to be done. So get out of your pyjamas and answer my email.

On top of the way the web has infiltrated our living spaces, we are actually being encouraged by web designers to think of it as a second home. During my Masters degree, I took an optional module in environmental psychology. I thought I was going to learn how to convince people to hug trees. But no, it has nothing to do with that, recycling or even sustainable homes. And I certainly had no idea that the University of Surrey is one of the leading institutions in the world on the subject. What environmental psychology is all about is how our physical environments influence us in ways we're not even aware of. It's the kind of course every town planner should take. It should be included in every architecture degree. No city would ever be blighted by those terrible cement egg boxes that were all the rage in the modernist 1960s and make city centres grim. Environmental psychologists believe human beings are at the centre of the physical world, and it shows how buildings, benches, parks and broken windows guide us from point A to point B.

So what on earth does this have to do with the web? Surprisingly and unexpectedly, taking this course opened up a little window of insight into how and why the web is becoming a place we call "home".

The woman who led the course was an academic named Gerda Speller. Her research looked at large-scale building projects – the ones when companies relocate people for safety's sake or because there's a national development that needs to go through their back gardens. She tries to explain to the companies and governments how they disrupt communities and transform relationships when they build replacement towns in a particular way. The collateral damage can be avoided, but often it's not. Gerda worked on the Eurotunnel project, following the people whose hometowns were destroyed as the rail link between London and Paris was built. She'd been called in to figure out which buildings in the new town should go where, how the roads should be built, what kinds of public spaces people would actually use and which to avoid in order to create a physical space. After all, these decisions make a difference in whether or not communities would reform among the newly displaced people. She'd also spent years researching a community in the north-east of England who'd had to be relocated after a closed mine nearby started spewing noxious gases. In both cases, centuries-old neighbourhood relationships fell apart, despite the efforts made by the planners to create new towns that were "people-centred".

There is an enigmatic and elusive, yet deliciously human, concept in environmental psychology: "place identity". When someone identifies with a place, they can become attached to it, and therefore want to be in it and part of it. They'll take care of it. They'll use it. They'll project themselves into the walls, park benches and public space. It's the difference between a house and a home: the building versus the warm and fuzzy place. The houses we rent or own can become homes after we've lived in them, we've painted them and we've remodelled them because, after all that effort and personalisation, we have saturated their walls with memories. We become comfortable in them as they become the backstage areas where we can let down our hair and be ourselves.

What Gerda and other environmental psychologists are expert at is understanding how spaces where people live and bounce through become the places that people feel ownership of and can identify with. Gerda looks at how public and private spaces are laid out rather than what their functions are intended to be, in order to unravel the emotional interaction we have with our surroundings. She uses this to describe how that can establish a sense of community: creating a location for accidental encounters in the street or building groups of park benches so they face inwards towards one another instead of outwards, away from one another. Place identities are essential qualities for both the success of spaces, houses and communities, and the psychological wellbeing of the individual.

Over the last 20 years, we have attuned ourselves to digital design. The architects of our physical worlds have always thought about how we navigate and consume their spaces, but now the designers of the cyberspaces that we traipse and surf through are starting to integrate similar ideas into websites. We call bits of the web "home" – literally, homepages that we decorate like the walls of a teenager's bedroom, personalising them with displays of who we are. Even on ready-made sites like Facebook, we still surround ourselves with the things that are meaningful to us by personalising our profiles. In two decades of web research, countless studies have described the ways people build online identities using text and multimedia in the same way that DIY junkies use paintbrushes and plasterboard. And when virtual places are infiltrated by hackers or ex-partners, they are considered spoiled and compromised and lose their psychological value. The sanctum is invaded and, as in the offline world, people move on, or they rebuild a relationship with that place.

"Home" isn't made of bricks and mortar, grass and mud, wood and straw. It is a de-physicalised, conceptual and psychological phenomenon. Technology is now an essential part of that. But once we grasp that distinction between the house and the emotional component that surrounds the most intimate part of our lives, we can easily see that the web can be just as much a home as the place where we lay our heads.

Favourites, avatars, aesthetic decisions – these all represent the person who "lives" there, so interaction designers try to create virtual places that have as much effect on pride, self-esteem and identity as the bricks and mortar places that their users live in. The science behind human–computer interaction – from systems that use eye-tracking to follow what we look at on a webpage to make what's on the site more interesting and compelling, to the mice, keyboards, track pads and Wiimotes we use to do things in the digital world – is there to make cyberspace feel more like a cyberplace.

LOL: THE INTERNET IS MADE OF CATS, AND OTHER MEMES

I love it when storytellers, whether they're telling their tales for television, radio, newspapers or books, share photos, notes, first drafts or anything that leads up to the finished product. These are behind-the-scenes glimpses into the thought processes that went into the creation of the finished product. They provide the context and extra dimension that brings a project alive for me as a reader, a viewer and an audience member. But this kind of self-exposure is rare, because so many creatives are obsessed with controlling their products and putting a glossy sheen on their creations. When I was filming for the BBC's *The Virtual Revolution*, apart from presenting the series itself, I was documenting the process with photos and a video diary – the first time a BBC series had done this. The director of photography caught me uploading something to the photo-sharing site Flickr and asked a very simple question, "Why?"

For him and the rest of the crew, I was doing a lot of extra work that was distracting from the real reason we were there. Our objective was to tell the story, and to do it from our point of view. But storytelling is evolving. Modern media consumers live in an overwhelmingly interactive world which is changing how we create and consume culture in the age of the web.

For a start, the ways in which we tell stories are evolving. Constant connectedness and new "companion" devices like tablets and mobile phones mean that we as audiences are now actively involved in the storytelling act. According to a survey for the Edinburgh Television Festival in 2011, more than half of us are "almost always" or "frequently" online while watching a TV show. The figure leaps to almost 97% of 18–24-year-olds. We're live tweeting, responding to what's happening on screen, writing and sharing our own versions and, in some cases, directing where the TV show goes. This means there are enormous opportunities to extend stories in all kinds of different, interactive ways. It also means that there are far more potential authors who want to have a say in what it is storytellers are telling.

Naturally, audiences still want a good yarn, but now we also want to be part of the experience itself. We want the sense that we are leading the action, that we are the heroes, that we are inherently involved in the story arc. We want our interests and beliefs to have an impact on what happens and we want to share this with our friends. This "participatory culture", says Professor Henry Jenkins from the University of Southern California, has implications for education, politics, participation and knowledge. And a digitally savvy cabal is indeed creating a form of storytelling that places the audience at the very heart of the action. These are people who grew up with interactive technology. They're kids with no experience and a cheap digital camera, or they're grownups at publishing organisations who have budgets to create or commission new kinds of stories.

Some of the new model storytellers have taken their inspirations from Kit Williams' 1979 book *Masquerade*, a picture book that captivated a generation of people, who pored over illustrations in the hopes of finding clues that would lead them to a treasure buried in the British Midlands. Others are inspired by the *Choose Your Own Adventure* stories, a series of books from the 1980s that gave the reader control over whether a character went in one direction ("turn to page 33") or another ("turn to page 42") at crucial turning points. Modern stories can now start anywhere: they're woven through blogs, magazine ads, TV slots, fashion labels and public phone boxes in the middle of a busy downtown neighbourhood. Clues to the next part of the adventure are littered across the physical world and in the virtual world. Consumers simply need to be tuned in to see them, and willing to take part in the unfolding narrative. The "Lost Experience", created by the people behind the hit ABC TV series *Lost*, told the TV series' backstory by planting a message in an ad for a car in *People* magazine, broadcasting a fake advert during the commercial break in the first episode of the fourth series, and leaving a garbled answering machine message at the other end of the telephone line. The people who wanted to find out more about the relationships between the main characters, plus information about a plotline that would be revealed in a later series, tapped into this and followed the Experience. The people who didn't could watch the television programmes and be none the wiser.

Frank Rose, author of *The Art of Immersion: How the Digital Generation is Remaking Hollywood, Madison Avenue and the Way We Tell Stories*, believes this is exactly what people want from their story experience. "The kind of multi-way conversation that the web makes possible is what we've always wanted to do," he says. "The technology finally enables it." Other creatives are using digital media to extend their storytelling palette in a similar way as Tom Stoppard did for Hamlet in *Rosencrantz and Guildenstern are Dead. Star Wars* creator George Lucas and *The Matrix* creators the Wachowskis have taken their cinematic plotlines across to other media – to TV, books and computer games – evolving minor characters and side stories in these different formats to enhance and expand on the original narrative, all while staying consistent to their story universes. In 2005, when the Morpheus character was killed off in the massively multiplayer online game version of *The Matrix*, that meant the end of the line for the character in all of the other spin-offs in the franchise too, including the comics and the animated series.

One of the most unexpected heroes of the global online scene is the cat. Seriously. "The internet is made of cats," *Huffington Post* co-founder Jonah Peretti once told me. They are the eternal subject of silly, one-click laugh fodder, from Maru, the Japanese YouTube kitty superstar most famous for jumping in and out of cardboard boxes (91 million views at the time of writing) to the cast of thousands of LOLCats – moggies photographed in compromising positions and labelled with poorly-spelled captions on icanhascheezburger.com and elsewhere. Although they may not provide as much of a moral compass as, say Cinderella or Little Red Riding Hood, they have as much global appeal as Mr Bean.

It's not surprising that much online content is comedy. The library of psychological and anthropological research describes humour as the glue that helps to define communities and keep them together. Psychologist Dr Rod Martin, who has published extensively on the role of humour in mental and physical health, describes it as a coping mechanism. We seek to establish a unified reality when we communicate with one another: when things have multiple interpretations or facts are fuzzy, we work together to define what the real story is. Along the way, we discover our inconsistencies and contradictions, and we use humour to poke fun and smooth over a molehill that could, without looking at the bright side, become a mountain.

Let's face it, LOLcats and a Japanese fat cat jumping into a box aren't exactly high brow. But across the ocean of possible new friends online, we need to find a way to establish connections and create common stories. We rely on universals. One of these, in the early 21st century, appears to be the cuteness of cats. Others are the people who become online celebrities. Those who find fame on the web – accidentally (like global singing sensation Susan Boyle) or through a carefully-orchestrated and well-placed social media campaign (like pop sensations Justin Bieber or Lady Gaga) – become a reference point for people's future stories, and part of a cultural conversation that can be a sophisticated, critical and positive force.

Human experience is a series of never-ending, overlapping stories bumping into one another in expected and unexpected ways. Our days are made up of personal narratives of good and evil, joy and conflict, and the real-life equivalents of magic potions and angry gnomes. We create our stories together, pushing and pulling based on how we interpret events, and what we project upon them. We analyse and synthesise the characters and events of our lives to help us make sense of the world. Storytellers are simply the people who piece together the elements of a yarn into a beginning, middle and end.

Stories are memory aids, instruction manuals and moral compasses. When they have been enlisted by charismatic leaders and turned into manifestos, dogmas and social policy, they have been the foundations for religions and political systems. When a storyteller has held a captive audience around a campfire, a cinema screen or on the page of a bestseller, they have reinforced local and universal norms about where we've been and where we're going. And when stories have been shared in the corner shop, at the pub or over dinner, they have helped us define who we are and how we fit in. But they way we spin them is changing.

Storytellers have always had to adapt their works when they've taken them to a different medium. A book needs to be rewritten before it becomes a movie; a newspaper article has to be adapted before it can be a radio programme; a TV show has to be rewritten before it becomes a computer game. Each of these platforms has things that they're better at doing than the others, and the web is no different. "We're in one of those 50-year windows when an entirely new medium is being created and no one knows what to do with it," says Frank Rose. Some people put themselves in the centre of the universe. Others let themselves be led. "All you can do is throw stuff out there and experiment," Rose says. We will continue to tell tales.

I remember several years ago, when the virtual world Second Life was the thing on the web, walking my avatar through an extraordinary representation of a cathedral. The frescoes, the stained glass and the flying buttresses were replicated to a degree that would make even the most cynical architect weep. Also enjoying the experience were 30 other virtual people from around the US and UK dressed in all manner of outerwear, from 1950s party dresses, via slinky black outfits with impossible heels, to squirrel costumes. They, as it turned out, were gathered in this cyberplace to celebrate a religious service.

I watched from the safe distance of a back-of-the-nave pew, listening to the officiant lead his flock through a traditional Catholic ceremony. I left after transubstantiation, just as they were processing in a typically sombre way to receive the Eucharist. A few months later, in the same virtual world, someone announced that they had experienced a virtual visitation: an innocuous digital object – a simulation of a piece of plywood – resembled the face of the Virgin Mary if you crossed your eyes and looked at it just so. I kid you not. There was a huge surge in new accounts as the faithful flocked in to see the miracle thing. And then someone bought it for $100. That's 100 real US dollars. It blew my mind.

The concept of religious ritual is so deeply embedded in our social fabric that it is natural for it to have made the leap to virtuality. People want to believe. Social networks like Facebook have active and close-knit communities of religious followers of all creeds, gathering in what science writer Margaret Wertheim described in her 1999 book *The Pearly Gates of Cyberspace* as "a new kind of realm for the mind". Perhaps, depending on your attitude to religion, it's more apt to describe these digital collectives in William Gibson's words again – a "consensual hallucination".

"Religion had two main purposes," the former Bishop of Edinburgh Richard Holloway explained to me on BBC Radio 4's *The Digital Human*. "The one is guidance: ways of trying to live well and wisely. Alongside that runs religion as explanation, as science." The reason Holloway feels the West is becoming increasingly secular is that the two functions overlap. "Religion got overtaken by real science."

God is most certainly not dead online, however. The web is littered with replications of sacred spaces of every creed and faith, and He (or She, or It) is being released from traditional doctrine to become everything to everybody. "On the web, you're more easily able to find your tribe," says Professor Heidi Campbell, a researcher at Texas A&M University, whose most recent book, *When Religion Meets New Media*, looked at how Christian, Muslim, Hindu and Jewish communities engage with the web. However, she adds, "It's not the internet that's transformed religion. There are larger social trends and processes at work." The web simply helps push those trends forward.

If football can be a religion for some, it seems so can the web. In 2011, technologist Jim Gilliam announced to a roomful of his peers, "The internet is my religion." Far from being a sacrilegious statement, Gilliam, a true believer in a Christian god, was describing his relationship with a technology that makes him feel connected to a whole far greater than just himself. And he believes many of his generation feel this too:

"What the people in this room do is spiritual and profound," he said to an audience of, at his admission, ordinarily cynical people. Yet as he continued there were murmurs of understanding and support in the crowd: "We are the leaders of this new religion. We have faith that people, connected, can create a new world. Each one of us is a creator but together we are the Creator."

And, boy, did that strike a chord. Jim's speech tapped into an early 21st-century need for meaning and community, a phenomenon that comes around every thousand years or so, and made him an overnight sensation in the technology community. The reason why what he said went down so well, even in a tough crowd of non-believers, is because he was preaching to a converted audience of geeks just like him who believe in the web, believe in its power, and are themselves seeking something. The faith these people have in the machine is like a pseudo-religious experience. To them, the web offers guidance and explanation: it generates a sense of belonging and provides interpretations for things that seem to make no sense, and meaning for things without context. Gilliam's turn of phrase simply translated what they were all feeling, and them into true believers.

The importance of the web in everyday life – from banking, to shopping, to socialising – means that religious organisations recognise that they have to take their churches and temples online in order to stay relevant and to be where the people are. Religious leaders have websites, blogs and Twitter feeds, and there are email prayerlines and online confessionals, as well as social networks for yogis and apps that call the faithful to prayer. "Being web-savvy should be a required skill for religious leaders," says Sister Catherine Wybourne, Prioress of the Holy Trinity Monastery in Oxfordshire, and @DigitalNun on Twitter.

Evangelicals, who have historically been keen to get their message out via whatever communication conduit is available, were the first organised religious groups to embrace the web, and non-traditional or sidelined religious movements made early forays online to get their version of the Word out. In contrast, Islam and Catholicism, which both place an emphasis on shared place in their rituals, have been the most hesitant. The mode through which their dogma is translated, traditionally text or spoken word, is tantamount, and technology is viewed as something more commercial rather than spiritual. "The web may have encouraged a lowest-common-denominator eclecticism and turned us into consumers of religion," argues Sister Catherine.

"I think that the openness of the internet works against [organized] religions," explains philosophy Professor Daniel Dennett. Dennett joins Richard Dawkins, Sam Harris and Christopher Hitchens as one of the Four Horsemen of the New Atheism: "I think they may be too exposed to grow beyond a certain point." What has traditionally been behind closed doors in ecclesiastical councils is now online, challenging the control that leaders once had over doctrine, and their flocks.

Just as the printing press ushered in the Reformation in the 16th century, because people could access religious texts for themselves and distribute their interpretations widely, the web has enabled the proliferation of different interpretations and articulations of religions, and we have witnessed the emergence of new communities and faiths. Individuals now have much more choice about who to approach as a source of authority. "Those people may have official, traditional credentials, or they may be Rabbi Google," says Professor Campbell.

"Religious leaders will have to get used to the idea of being more accountable and more transparent in their dealings and having to engage, on equal terms, with those who stand outside the traditional hierarchies," says Sister Catherine. Despite all of this, the web has not increased inter-faith communication. As with politics, birds of a feather flock together. "Unless you're looking for diversity, you're not going to find it online," says Campbell. Indeed, Wertheim believes that the differences between religions are actually amplified online.

What about the web itself as a religion, as proclaimed by internet apostle Gilliam? Well, there is a school of thought, not a religion, that is promoted by a flock of influential technologists and science fiction writers like Ray Kurtzweil and Vernor Vinge, and supported by several wealthy business people, that predicts a rapture-like event in which the network itself becomes sentient. In "the Singularity," computational power will reach such a capacity that it will achieve greater-than-human intelligence. Because the rate of change is so rapid – exponential, according to Moore's Law, a concept that describes technological capability doubling every two years – so-called "superintelligences" are expected to design ever-increasing intelligences by themselves that will quickly surpass unaided human intelligence. And because we can't comprehend what these intelligences will be without the aid of technology, we have no idea what will happen. Rather like the Second Coming.

Many of this school of thought's founders struck it big as businesspeople in the first dotcom boom, and are using their substantial disposable capital to support the Singularity. In fact, members of the general public can sign up for a very expensive series of courses at a dedicated "University" in Silicon Valley to "focus on solving the planet's most pressing challenges using exponential and accelerating technologies". Graduate students, business executives and medical professionals can attend courses with an impressive roster of forward-thinking faculty members, including former astronauts, directors at some of Silicon Valley's biggest companies, and entrepreneurs. Like L. Ron Hubbard's modern belief system, Scientology, the Singularity has some high-level proponents, and their ideas are compelling to people who seek them.

There has yet to be an online-only religion that has any resilience, however. "Gilliam's speech struck chords with a community of people who share an enthusiasm for the embrace of online connectedness," says religious scholar and Episcopal priest Akma Adam. "That alone as a basis of self-understanding of religion is missing some aspect of what would make a more durable religious identification." So while the internet takes over much of our lives, and offers those with an existing faith a compelling arena to meet other worshippers, we have yet to see a true, internet-only religion come forth. This may, of course, simply be a matter of time: we just haven't had the requisite number of years. But no matter how enthusiastic about technology some people might get – and the behaviour of fans of certain computer manufacturers does approach a fervour that resembles a religious ecstasy – this enthusiasm cannot be completely compared to a fully-rounded offline religion with all of its durable cultural and organisational hierarchies. The web has not transformed faith, but religious-like behaviour might have, miraculously, changed the web.

UNTANGLING
THE FUTURE

In the 13 years since the research that has become this book began, more than 1.5 billion people have logged on to the web for the first time, trebling the digital population. The web has evolved from an information resource to a place of self-expression and revolution. And, out of all the possible directions in which it could have gone, we have done a very human thing: we've coalesced around one search engine, one social network and one online marketplace.

We use the web to express our selves, our social worlds and our institutions. It is a resource for our cultures, our faiths and our identities. It is a platform for our economies, our places of work and our education systems. There is no one area of our lives that has not, in a large or small way, been entangled by the web, and yet, as this book has shown, in many ways the web has failed to transform us. Instead, we have imported ourselves and our social systems into the machine.

There is one more area that that requires our attention: how web technologies will drive the future. They won't just reflect who we are; they'll make us who we are. There are countless philosophy and computer science departments in hundreds of universities around the world full of the cleverest people imaginable, all working on digital technologies that can mimic human processes like learning and logic. That's one kind of artificial intelligence. But what it feels like to be a social and psychological human cannot, at the moment, be replicated. If the technologists have their way, that will change. They will replicate us entirely.

IDEOLOGIES OF
THE TECHNOLOGIES

People generally don't think of the paper on which the daily news is printed, or the printing press that puts it there, as being anything but neutral. They identify the publishers as the ideologues and the medium as a conduit. You'd think the same, broadly speaking, would apply where the web is concerned: Julian Assange didn't invent the wiki platform where the confidential wires were leaked, he was the editor and WikiLeaks was the medium. But in *Consent of the Networked*, former CNN China Bureau Chief Rebecca MacKinnon offers a reality check: "We have a problem," she writes. "We understand how power works in the physical world, but we do not yet have a clear understanding of how power works in the digital realm." In fact, we probably don't even think about power when we update our statuses on Twitter, connect with old school friends and upload pictures to Facebook, buy a book based on a recommendation from Amazon or use Mail, Docs, Plus, Maps or Search on Google.

The truth is that software, from computer games to web services, from Amazon to Match.com, is suffused with the principles decreed by the context in which it is produced. "Technology is neither good nor bad, nor is it neutral," says Kranzberg's First Law of Technology. Spaces like Facebook, places like Second Life or World of Warcraft and technologies like Google permit and discourage certain kinds of uses, and these are being determined by the people behind the machines. The ways in which these web services fulfil our needs to connect, play or search for information and products are coloured by their developers' personal backgrounds, life circumstances, social circles, hometowns, financial wealth and many other things. We are critical of the news we read, the programmes we watch, the movies we see and the art we appreciate. We are aware that they are constructs of their creators. We can point to liberal newspapers and conservative TV. We can name a Spielberg film and a Warhol print. Yet we seem to forget that the web is a network that is entirely human-produced, and primarily created by people who live in a small area of Northern California.

The architecture of the internet and the designs of the web systems we use are the scaffolding upon which the people in charge of the new world – Google creators Larry Page and Sergey Brin and Facebook CEO Mark Zuckerberg in the West; the creators of social networks Renren and mixi, blogging software Sina Weibo, search engine Baidu and others in the East; the architects of money-exchange system M-Pesa in Africa – are using their agendas to establish how we do all of the things that I've discussed in this book. These agendas, which they may or may not be aware of, shape the information we receive and how we make sense of it.

Almost imperceptibly, software giant Google has integrated itself into the fabric of our daily lives: we use it to find and track news and information, to connect with friends, to increase our productivity, to locate us in both the physical and the virtual worlds. With all this ephemeral and seemingly disconnected data, the company delivers the human value, "relevance". It tells us what is the most appropriate information that will serve our needs. It has become our window to the world of knowledge.

Google's mission is "to organise the world's knowledge and make it universally accessible and useful". And here's the most important bit of this statement: "make it [...] useful". After all, Google's ability to deliver a useful thing that solved your problem is what made it the market leader. How Google judges "usefulness" is programmed into the computer code that gives us search results. As Ken Auletta explained in his book *Googled*, information's "usefulness" depends on how often a site has been linked to on the web, the number of times it's been clicked on by users who've searched for similar information, and whether the information comes from a "reliable" source. There are human value judgments in each of these core components. Someone at some point had to make a decision about them in order to program them in. And this is what we should be aware of: Google doesn't deliver us information that's independent. It is a cyborg: part machine, part human. It filters our problems through a technological system that is, at its most basic level, subjective.

First, the importance placed on the number of links to a site stems from the philosophy that the crowd is always wise. Sure, it can be. But groupthink can also lead to dangerous booms and busts, like the South Sea Bubble, Tulip mania, or the recent US mortgage crisis. As long ago as 1841, the author Charles MacKay worried about the "madness of crowds".

Second, the infinite loop of feedback from other Google users based on "similarity" assumes that what you do online is "you". What you search for, what you say in an email, where you go, what you watch and who you hang out with of course don't capture the whole you, just as who you are at work is different from who you are at home, but this whole "you" is still used to judge whether you are "similar" to someone else.

Your similarity to another person is based on the information you give to a system, and how well that matches the information it holds about other people. But there are value judgments implicit in this process too. Google puts you into categories it has devised based on what you've searched for, what you've looked at on YouTube, what you've said in an email and what you've written in a document. It looks for particular keywords, and reduces these things into lists that a machine can read. It's easy for the machine to get it wrong.

The last way Google decides what's relevant is the one that's laden with the most personal bias. It's based on the ranking given to sources of information. It would rank a site like the *New York Times* higher than Jane Blogger's homepage, even though the *New York Times* might be using Jane Blogger's homepage as its source. This judgment exposes who the search engine believes has a more credible and reliable voice. If that's the case, it becomes important to know what its other, informal boardroom motto, "Don't be evil", means. What is "evil" to a company that gave information on searchers to the US National Security Agency in 2010, and in 2011 pulled out of China because it didn't want to comply with that government's surveillance state?

The politics of the web, and the people who build it, are bubbling just under the surface.

As I have said before, the web has not changed our fundamental needs. We still express who we are, and try to fit in. But people are in danger of becoming "techno-fundamentalists". This is Siva Vaidhyanathan's description of people who blindly accept what they are delivered, invisible risks and all. And this is why we are afraid of what the web is doing to us: we worry we've placed too much faith in the machine. We feel disempowered, and that we have lost control.

How do we avoid falling into a techno-fundamentalist trap? By understanding what the people who are creating the tools believe is "human" and then measuring that against our own views.

Software companies like Google, Facebook, Twitter and the others are limited by the fact that they have to construct an online version of humanity using binary code. They are forced, by the available technology, to reduce the fulfilment of trust, desire, belonging, emotion and identity into 1s and 0s. Throughout this book, I've described how complex those are and how we as users import ourselves into the web, despite the technological shortcomings.

Technology can't (currently) get people to have insight or attribute value, in spite of its attempts to do so, and there is no one-size-fits-all solution, despite what developers would like to believe. It would be like trying to program love, or grace, or elegance. There are so many things involved, it would fill up a psychology textbook. But even by saying that they wish to predict these kinds of extraordinary human phenomena using software, this opens a window into what the people in charge of the new world think humanity is: predictable and, frankly, rather dumb. This is something we have to contend with as critical adults, but what about kids at school age who are learning that digital technologies are just another thing they have to read to understand a complex concept, like a textbook or an educational film? A rich stream of interactive educational tools are being integrated into classrooms around the world: computer games. In 2006, I wrote a white paper for the computer games industry, explaining how their "entertainment" was being adopted for more serious purposes. "Play has historically been acknowledged as an important part of learning, and has been present in learning environments through simulations, role plays and quizzes," says the report. "As digital versions of play have evolved, interactivity-savvy entrepreneurs, professionals, academics and teachers have naturally introduced the palette of technologies afforded them by the modern world into formal and informal learning spaces." These are the folk who played games in their youth and realised their potential. They are people who are using the web to teach kids about genetics, self-confidence and sex, making online worlds to teach narrative and creative writing, and simulation games to teach them about town planning and economic models.

But importing off-the-shelf commercial products into classrooms does pose a few problems, whether it's World of Warcraft or Facebook: first, it assumes that teachers understand the software and how to use it. There's often a knowledge gap, imagined or real, that makes many teachers wary in case the students have to teach *them* what to do. Second, it also assumes that students understand the software and how to use it. There's an expectation that kids will intuitively know, but not every kid has equal access to these kinds of things at home, nor do all kids take to them in the same way and at the same pace.

Then the content of games needs to be reckoned with. Their creators most likely didn't have education objectives in mind when they were trying to create their blockbusters. When teachers are using World of Warcraft to teach their students about group dynamics and resource management, they're dealing with economic and social systems that may work in the game world, but don't have all of the complexities of, say, Keynesian economic theory. Students would obviously be shortchanged if they thought the economic principles were the same, but games, as well as social networks and online communities, can be useful entry points for difficult concepts. A bit like Wikipedia.

How might the web have been different if any of the other web-like technologies that were being developed at the same time had been successful? "The fateful, unnerving aspect of information technology is that a particular design will occasionally happen to fill a niche and, once implemented, turn out to be unalterable, even though a better design might just as well have taken its place before the moment of entrenchment," says polemicist and web developer Jaron Lanier. Web founder Tim Berners-Lee's original intent was to create a system that served a community of physicists, Lanier reminds us. It wasn't intended to serve the whole world.

Rather than asking, "What is the web doing to us?" as individuals, as communities and as a society, perhaps, when we use it to fulfil our needs, we should remember that it ultimately reflects our humanity in its barest sense. We should instead be asking two other questions: "What does what we're doing online say about us?" and "What does it mean?"

REFERENCES

This is not a complete list of references, but a compendium of the academic research I used in the chapters of this book. For a complete list of references, including non-academic articles, blogposts, interviews, videos, images and other sources, go to http://untanglingtheweb.tumblr.com

Adamic, L. A. & Glance, N. (2005) The political blogosphere and the 2004 US election: Divided they blog. Proceedings of the 3rd international workshop on Link discovery, pp. 36–43.

Adamic, L. A., Lento, T. M. & Fiore, A. T. (2012) How you met me. ICWSM '12 short paper.

Arnold, M. (2004) The connected home: probing the effects and affects of domesticated ICTs. In Artful Integration: Interweaving media, materials and practices (vol. 2). Proceedings of the Eighth Biennial Participatory Design Conference (27–31 July 2004).

Attwood, F. (2010) *Porn.com*. Peter Lang.

Bargh, J. A., McKenna, K. Y. A. & Fitzsimons, G. M. (2002) Can you see the real me? Activation and expression of the "true self" on the internet. *Journal of Social Issues*, 58(1), 33–48.

Barlow, J. P. (1993) Selling wine without bottles: The economy of mind on the global net. EFF. At http://w2.eff.org/Misc/Publications/John_Perry_Barlow/HTML/idea_economy_article.html.

Bell, G. (2011) Life, death, and the iPad: Cultural symbols and Steve Jobs. *Communications of the ACM*, 54(12), 24–25.

Berman, J. & Bruckman, A. S. (2001) The Turing game: Exploring identity in an online environment. *Convergence*, 7(3), 83–102.

Bhal, K. T & Leekha, N. D. (2007) Exploring cognitive moral logics using grounded theory: The case of software piracy. *Journal of Business Ethics*, 81(3), 635–646.

Bilstad, B. T. (1996) Obscenity and indecency on the usenet: The legal and political future of alt.sex.stories. *Journal of Computer-Mediated Communication*, 2(2).

Block, J. J. (2008) Issues for *DSM-IV*: Internet addiction. *The American Journal of Psychiatry*, 165, 306–307.

Bowker, N. & Tuffin, K. (2003) Dicing with deception: People with disabilities' strategies for managing safety and identity online. *Journal of Computer-Mediated Communication*, 8(2).

Brasher, B. E. (2001) *Give Me That Online Religion*. Rutgers University Press.

Brown, P. & Minty, J. (2006) Media coverage and charitable giving after the 2004 tsunami. William Davidson Institute Working Paper No. 855. At http://ssrn.com/abstract=968760.

Bunt, G. (2009) *iMuslims: Rewiring the House of Islam*. UNC Press.

Cameron, S. & Fox, M. (2011) Working from home: Leisure gain or leisure loss? In S. Cameron (ed.), *Handbook on the Economics of Leisure*. Edward Elgar Publishing, pp. 128–152.

Cassidy, W. P. (2007) Online news credibility: An examination of the perceptions of newspaper journalists. *Journal of Computer-Mediated Communication*, 12(2), 478–498.

Castronova, E. (2002) On virtual economies. CESifo Working Paper Series No. 752. At http://ssrn.com/abstract=338500.

Coombs, R. H. & Kenkel, W. F. (1966) Sex differences in dating aspirations and satisfaction with computer-selected partners. *Journal of Marriage & Family*, 1, 62–66.

Cooper, A., Delmonico, D. L. & Burg, R. (2000) Cybersex users, abusers, and compulsives: New findings and implications. *Sexual Addiction and Compulsivity*, 7(5), 5–29.

Cummings, A. S. (2010) From monopoly to intellectual property: Music piracy and the remaking of American copyright, 1909–1971. *The Journal of American History*, 659–681.

Debatin, B., Lovejoy, J. P., Horn, A.-K., & Hughes, B. N. (2009) Facebook and online privacy: Attitudes, behaviors, and unintended consequences. *Journal of Computer-Mediated Communication*, 15(1), 83–108.

Deutsch, M. & Gerard, H. B. (1955) A study of normative and informational social influences upon individual judgment. *The Journal of Abnormal and Social Psychology*, 51(3), 629–636.

Diakopolous, N. & Naaman, M. (2011) Towards quality discourse in online news comments. Proceedings of the ACM 2011 Conference on Computer Supported Cooperative Work. New York.

Dingfelder, S. F. (2011) Reflecting on narcissism: Are young people more self-obsessed than ever before? *Monitor on Psychology*, 42(2).

Douglas, K. (2007) Psychology, discrimination and hate groups online. In A. Joinson, K. McKenna, T. Postmes & U.-D. Reips (eds), *The Oxford Handbook of Internet Psychology*. Oxford University Press, pp. 155–163.

Dutta, S., Dutton, W. H. & Law, G. (2011) The new internet world: A global perspective on freedom of expression, privacy, trust and security online. INSEAD working paper 2011/89/TOM.

Dutton, W. H., Helsper, E. J., Whitty, M. T., Li, N., et al. (2009) The role of the internet in reconfiguring marriages: A cross-national study. *Interpersona*, 3(2), 3–18.

Eisenstein, E. L. (1994) *The Printing Press as an Agent of Change*. Cambridge University Press.

Ess, C. (2007) Cross-cultural perspectives on religion and computer-mediated communication. *Journal of Computer-Mediated Communication*, 12(3), 9.

Eysenbach, G., Powell, J., Englesakis, M., Rizo, C., et al. (2004) Health-related virtual communities and electronic support groups: Systematic review of the effects of online peer to peer interactions. *British Medical Journal*, 328(7449), 1166.

Foot, K., Warnick, B. & Schneider, S. M. (2005) Web-based memorializing after September 11: Toward a conceptual framework. *Journal of Computer-Mediated Communication*, 11(1), 4.

Fowler, D. (2008) *Youth Culture in Modern Britain, c.1920–c.1970*. Palgrave Macmillan.

Friedman, O. (2008) First possession: An assumption guiding information about who owns what. *Psychonomic Bulletin & Review*, 15(2), 290–295.

Garrison, B. (2001) Diffusion of online information technologies in newspaper newsrooms. *Journalism*, 2(2), 221–239.

Goggin, G. M. & Newell, C. (2002) Communicating disability: What's the matter with internet studies? In M. Power (ed.), *Refereed Articles from the Proceedings of the ANZCA 2002 Conference. Communication: Reconstructed for the 21st Century*, Coolangatta, 10–12 July.

Goldhaber, M. (1997) Attention economy and the net. *First Monday*, 2(4).

Gora, Y. (2009) ICT and effects on "togetherness" in family households. RMIT University/Smart Services Cooperative Research Centre.

Greenberg, S. & Neustaedter, C. (2011) Shared living, experiences and intimacy over video chat in long-distance relationships. Department of Computer Science, University of Calgary.

Gregory, C. (1989–1990) A willing suspension of disbelief. *The Student Historical Journal*, 21, Loyola University.

Gross, R. & Acquisti, A. (2005) Information revelation and privacy in online social networks. In WPES '05 Proceedings of the 2005 ACM Workshop on Privacy in the Electronic Society, New York.

Hart, A. (2004) The role of the internet in patient–practitioner relationships: Findings from a qualitative research study. *Journal of Medical Internet Research*, 6(3).

Hart, T. R. (2002) ePhilanthropy: Using the internet to build support. *International Journal of Nonprofit and Voluntary Sector Marketing*, 7(4), 353–360.

Haythornthwaite, C. (2007) Social networks and online community. In A. Joinson, K. McKenna, T. Postmes & U. Reips (eds), *The Oxford Handbook of Internet Psychology*. Oxford University Press.

Henwood, F., Wyatt, S., Hart, A. & Smith, J. (2003) "Ignorance is bliss sometimes": Constraints on the emergence of the "informed patient" in the changing landscapes of health information. *Sociology of Health & Illness*, 25(6), 589–607.

Higgs, K. (2010) EroTICs: The first findings. Association for Progressive Communications.

Hodkinson, P. (2007) Youth cultures: A critical outline of key debates. In P. Hodkinson & W. Deicke (eds), *Youth Cultures: Scenes, Subcultures and Tribes*. Routledge, pp. 1–23.

Hogan, B., Li, N. & Dutton, W. H. (2011) A global shift in the social relationships of networked individuals: Meeting and dating online comes of age. Oxford Internet Institute, University of Oxford.

Home Affairs Committee (2012) Roots of Violent Radicalisation. House of Commons, London.

Ibrahim, Y. (2008) The new risk communities: Social networking sites and risk. *International Journal of Media and Cultural Politics*, 4(2), 245–253.

Ito, M., Baumer, S., Bittanti, M, boyd, d., et al. (2010) *Hanging Out, Messing Around, and Geeking Out: Kids Living and Learning with New Media*. MIT Press.

Jakobsson, M. & Taylor, T. L. (2003) The sopranos meets EverQuest: Social networking in massively multiplayer online games. Melbourne DAC2003, Melbourne, Australia.

Jenkins, H. (2006) *Convergence Culture*. New York University Press.

Johnson, K. (2001) Media and social change: The modernizing influences of television in rural India. *Media Culture Society*, 23(2), 147–169.

Johnson, K. A. (2011) The effect of Twitter posts on students' perceptions of instructor credibility. *Learning, Media and Technology*, 36(1), 21–38.

Johnson, R. & Downing, L. H. (1979) Deindividuation and valence of cues: Effects on prosocial and antisocial behaviour. *Journal of Personality and Social Psychology*, 37(9), 1532–1538.

Jungnickel, K. & Bell, G. (2009) Home is where the hub is? Wireless infrastructures and the nature of domestic culture in Australia. In M. Foth (ed.), *Handbook of Research on Urban Informatics: Community Integration, Implementation*. IGI Global.

Kennedy, M. (1995) Charitable giving by individuals: A study of attitudes and practice. *Human Relations*, 48(6), 685–709.

Kjeldgaard, D. & Askegaard, S. (2006) The globalization of youth culture: The global youth segment as structures of common difference. *Journal of Consumer Research*, 33, 231–247.

Kraut, R., Patterson, M., Lundmarkm, V., Kiesler, S., et al. (1998) Internet paradox: A social technology that reduces social involvement and psychological well-being? *American Psychologist*, 53(9), 1017–1031.

Krotoski, A. (2004) Online games, offline selves: A possible selves approach to offline self-concept negotiation through play in massively multiplayer online role playing games. MSc thesis, Department of Psychology, School of Human Sciences, University of Surrey, UK.Krotoski, A. (2009) Social influence in Second Life: Social network and social psychological processes in the diffusion of belief and behaviour on the web. PhD dissertation, Department of Psychology, School of Human Sciences, University of Surrey, UK.

Lathouwers, K., de Moor, J. & Didden, R. (2009) Access to and use of the internet by adolescents who have a physical disability: A comparative study. *Research in Developmental Disabilities*, 30(4), 711–720.

Levine, D. (2000) Virtual attraction: What rocks your boat. *CyberPsychology & Behavior*, 3(4), 565–573.

Livingstone, S. (2008) Taking risky opportunities in youthful content creation: Teenagers' use of social networking sites for intimacy, privacy and self-expression. *New Media & Society*, 10(3), 393–411.

Livingstone, S., Hadon, L, Gorzif, A. & Olafsson, K. (2011) EU Kids Online. London School of Economics and Political Science.

Mankowski, E. & Rappaport, J. (1995) Stories, identity, and the psychological sense of community. In R. S. Wyer (ed.), *Advances in Social Cognition: The Real Story*. Routledge, pp. 221–226.

Manning, J. C. (2006) The impact of internet pornography on marriage and the family: A review of the research. *Sexual Addiction & Compulsivity*, 13, 131–165.

202   UNTANGLING THE WEB

Markus, H. & Nurius, P. (1986) Possible selves. *American Psychologist*, 41(9), 954–969.

Marshall, P. D. (2006) New media – new self: The changing power of celebrity. In P. D. Marshall (ed.), *The Celebrity Culture Reader*. Routledge.

Mayer-Schönberger, V. (2010) *Delete: The Virtue of Forgetting in the Digital Age*. Princeton University Press.

McLuhan, M. (1962) *The Gutenberg Galaxy: The Making of Typographic Man*. University of Toronto Press.

Moore, M. (2010) Shrinking world: The decline of international reporting in the British press. Media Standards Trust.

Oboler, A. (2008) The rise and fall of a Facebook hate group. *First Monday*, 13(11).

Ochs, E., Taylor, C., Rudolph, D. & Smith, R. (1992) Storytelling as a theory-building activity. *Discourse Processes*, 15(1), 37–72.

Opir, E., Nass, C. & Wagner, A. D. (2009) Cognitive control in media multitaskers. *Proceedings of the National Academy of Sciences*, 106(37), 15583–15587.

Park, Y., Lim, C. & Nam, T. (2010) CheekTouch: An affective interaction technique while speaking on the mobile phone. CHI 2012, 10–15 April 2010, Atlanta, GA.

Parkes, C. M., Laungani, P. & Young, B. (1997) *Death and Bereavement Across Cultures*. Psychology Press.

Paumgarden, N. (2001) Looking for someone: Sex, love, and loneliness on the Internet. *The New Yorker*. At http://www.newyorker.com/reporting/2011/07/04/110704fa_fact_paumgarten.

Pierce, J. L., Kostova, T. & Dirks, K. Y. (2003) The state of psychological ownership: Integrating and extending a century of research. *Review of General Psychology*, 7(1), 84–107.

Pitsillides, S. Katsikides, S. & Conreen, M. (2009) Digital death, "Images of virtuality: Conceptualizations and applications in everyday life". An IFIP WG9.5 "Virtuality and Society" international workshop, 23–24 April, Athens.

Proshansky, H. M (1978) The city and self-identity. *Environment and Behavior*, 10(2), 147–169.

Radovanovic, D. & Ragnedda, M. (2012) Small talk in the digital age: Making sense of phatic posts. Proceedings of the #MSM2012 workshop, 16 April 2012, Lyon, France.

Rainie, L., Horrigan, J., Wellman, B. & Boase, J. (2006) The Strength of Internet Ties. Pew Internet & American Life Project.

Rod, M. A. (2007) *The Psychology of Humor: An Integrative Approach*. Academic Press.

Rose, F. (2001) *The Art of Immersion*. W.W. Norton & Company.

Saillie, G. & Gustavel, J. (1988) The effects of hypertext on reader knowledge representation. *Proceedings of the Human Factors and Ergonomics Society Annual Meeting*, 5, 296–300.

Sheehan, B., Tsao, J. & Yang, S. (2011) Motivations for gratifications of digital music piracy among college students. *Atlantic Journal of Communication*, 18, 241–258.

Sheehan, K. B. & Hoy, M. G. (2000) Dimensions of privacy concern among online consumers. *Journal of Public Policy & Marketing*, 19(1), 62–73.

Simmel, G. (1978) *The Philosophy of Money* (3rd edn). Routledge.

Smith, J. R. & McSweeny, A. (2007) Charitable giving: The effectiveness of a revised theory of planned behaviour model in predicting donating intentions and behaviour. *Journal of Community & Applied Social Psychology*, 17(5), 363–386.

Sparrow, B., Liu, J. & Wegner, D. M. (2011) Google effects on memory: Cognitive consequences of having information at our fingertips. *Science*, 333(6043), 776–778.

Standage, T. (1998) *The Victorian Internet*. The Berkeley Publishing Group.

Sugarman, B. (1967) Involvement in youth culture, academic achievement and conformity in school: An empirical study of London schoolboys. *British Journal of Sociology*, 18(1967), 151–164, 317.

Suler, J. (2004) The online disinhibition effect. *CyberPsychology & Behavior*, 7(3), 321–326.

Swinyard, W. R., Rinne, H. & Keng Kau, A. (1990) The morality of software piracy: A cross-cultural analysis. *Journal of Business Ethics*, 9(8), 655–664.

Talamo, A. & Ligorio, B. (2001) Strategic identities in cyberspace. *CyberPsychology and Behavior*, 4(1), 109–122.

Van Alstyne, M. & Brynjolfsson, E. (1996) *Electronic Communities: Global Village or Cyberbalkans?*, MIT Press.

Walter, T., Hourizi, R., Moncur, W. & Pitsillides, S. (2011) Does the internet change how we die and mourn? An overview. *Omega: Journal of Death and Dying*, 64(4), 275–302.

Wellman B., Smith, A., Wells, A. & Kennedy, T. (2008) Networked Families. Pew Internet & American Life Project.

Wertheim, M. (1999) *The Pearly Gates of Cyberspace: A History of Space from Dante to the Internet*. W.W. Norton & Company.

Westin, A. F. (2003) Social and political dimensions of privacy. *Journal of Social Issues*, 59(2).

White, D. S. & Le Cornu, A. (2011) Visitors and residents: A new typology for online engagement. *First Monday*, 16(9).

White, M. & Dorman, S. M. (2001) Receiving social support online: Implications for health education. *Health Education Research*, 16(6), 693–707.

White, R. W. & Horvitz, E. (2008) Cyberchondria: Studies of the escalation of medical concerns in web search. Microsoft Research.

White, R. W. & Horvitz, E. (2009) Experiences with web search on medical concerns and self-diagnosis. Proceedings of the Annual Symposium of the American Medical Informatics Association (AMIA 2009).

Whitty, M. (2007) Love letters: the development of romantic relationships throughout the ages. In A. Joinson, K. McKenna, T. Postmes & U. Reips (eds), *The Oxford Handbook of Internet Psychology*. Oxford University Press.

Whitty, M. & Buchanan, T. (2009) Looking for love in so many places: Characteristics of online daters and speed daters. *Interpersona*, 3(2).

Whitty, M. & Buchanan, T. (2012) The online dating romance scam: A serious crime. *Cyberpsychology, Behavior, and Social Networking*, 15(3), 181–183.

Whitty, M., Buchanan, T. & Watson, A. (2009) *LoveGeist: Love Landscape*. Match International.

Wojcieszak, M. (2008) False consensus goes online. *Public Opinion Quarterly*, 72(4), 781–791.

Young, K. S. (1999) Internet addiction: Symptoms, evaluation and treatment. In L. VandeCreek & T. L. Jackson (eds), *Innovations in Clinical Practice* (vol. 17). Professional Resource Press.

INDEX